Education
in the 18th Century

Publications of
the McMaster University
Association for 18th-Century Studies

Copies of all volumes are available from Garland Publishing, Inc.

Education
in the 18th Century

Editor-in-Chief
J. D. Browning

Garland Publishing, Inc.
New York & London
1979

The Association for 18th-Century Studies

McMaster University
Hamilton, Ontario
Canada

Editorial Board:

Chairman: John D. Browning

Paul S. Fritz   César Rouben

James King   Robert Van Dusen

The members of the committee wish to express their gratitude to
McMaster University for its continuing and generous support of
the Association and all of its activities.

Library of Congress Cataloging in Publication Data

Main entry under title:
Education in the 18th century.

(Publications of the McMaster University
Association for 18th-Century studies ; v. 7)
1. Education—Europe—History—18th century—
Addresses, essays, lectures.   2. Education—
Europe—Philosophy—History—18th century—
Addresses, essays, lectures.   3. Enlightenment—
Addresses, essays, lectures.   I. Browning, John D.
II. Series: McMaster University Association
for 18th-Century Studies. Publications ; v. 7.
LA621.5.E38   370'.9'033   79-18182
ISBN 0-8240-4006-6

Printed on acid-free, 250-year-life paper
Manufactured in the United States of America

Contents

Introduction

Writing on education, Grimm spluttered in 1762, "is the mania of the year." The crotchety journalist-baron was, in fact, not too far off the mark. Indeed, the eighteenth century as a whole evidenced a fascination with education that was unprecedented in its intensity.

The papers in the present volume examine this multifaceted topic from a variety of aspects. Essays by Lewis Beck, Samuel Ajzenstat and James Noxon analyze the educational thought of two of the leading philosophers of the age, Kant and Hume. James Leith looks at educational theory from a different perspective, exploring the ideas and proposals of the less well known authors of educational tracts in France in the years prior to the Revolution. Two papers focus on education in practice during the late seventeenth and early eighteenth centuries. Edward Gregg's essay inquires into the royal upbringing of Queen Anne and her contemporaries, while James King investigates the early schooling of Alexander Pope, an English Roman Catholic. Finally, in his study of the Paris Hôtel-Dieu, Louis S. Greenbaum discusses the consequences of the introduction of a new form of medical education for French physicians and surgeons.

That the eighteenth century devoted so much attention to the problem of education is perhaps not surprising. It was an age of crisis, when new currents of thought were challenging intellectuals to examine their most fundamental assumptions and to rethink traditional beliefs. The Enlightenment reopened the question of the essential nature of man, and with it, as a corollary, the question of how he should be educated. The century, heir to the scientific revolution, was also an age of optimism, when planning for the future seemed a valid, even an essential, activity. If man had, as many philosophes suggested, the capacity for self-improvement and the potential to control and modify his social environment, then he enjoyed phenomenal power and bore tremendous responsibility. Not only did he have to decide what the characteristics of regenerated man and his transformed society should be, but he had to determine how these attributes and conditions could most effectively be brought into being.

Careful education of the young seemed the obvious answer. The thinkers of the eighteenth century were not, of course, the first to assume that the mind of the child was the key to the society of tomorrow. Nor was their faith in education new. Plato, the humanists, the Germans of the Protestant Reformation, and the Jesuits had all in turn extolled the power of education and attempted to harness it to their own ends. But the conviction that education was the solution to the woes of society was significantly strengthened in the eighteenth century by the support that science, especially the infant science of psychology, seemed to bring to traditional beliefs about the influence of education, and by the rejection on the part of many thinkers of the doctrine of original sin. If a child's ideas were nothing more than the sum total of the sensations which acted upon him, then a systematic manipulation of his environment should result in an adult possessing predictable beliefs. Furthermore, if the child was not an intrinsically wicked being, dependent upon divine intervention to rescue him from the forces of evil, if instead he was a blank slate waiting to be written upon, then his potential for perfection was presumably unlimited. A properly designed program of instruction and training, conscientiously applied, should produce that superior being who would in turn make possible the superior society.

In its crudest and most simplistic form the Enlightenment doctrine of education taught that the child was a lump of wax that could be moulded into whatever shape one wanted and programmed with whatever beliefs and ideas one deemed desirable. Certainly writer after writer proposed systems and propounded methods based on these assumptions. But to dismiss eighteenth-century educational thought as so naively optimistic and so unquestioningly self-confident would be to do it a serious injustice. Many thinkers were wrestling with the broader problems of morality and human freedom, and these concerns were reflected in the debate on education. Rousseau, for example, whose *Emile* evoked a tremendous response in England and Germany as well as in France, was agonizingly concerned with how the moral freedom of mankind, which he saw existing in the state of nature, could be preserved in a social setting. Like many of his contemporaries, he was unable to accept the ultimate conclusion of the Lockean thesis that man was born without any innate moral propensities. Young Emile has natural instincts to goodness and his education, in its earliest stages, is simply their unfolding independent of, and protected from, the pressures of society. As Emile grows older his mentor is permitted to encourage and utilize these moral propensities in order to ensure his development into a virtuous adult.

Not all who rejected Locke's *tabula rasa* were as sanguine as Rousseau about the essential nature of the child, however. Many felt he was born with instincts to both good and evil. They envisaged the educator's task as one of mobilizing and strengthening the pupil's moral tendencies while simultaneously suppressing and counteracting the immoral which might otherwise seize control. The pessimistic underside of the educational literature is the overwhelming fear on the part of some that only constant care and attention could prevent the forces of evil from predominating, that education, even at its best, was not foolproof.

The question of morality, what it was, and how it might be encouraged, was thus a central concern of many educational theorists, as it was of the Enlightenment as a whole. The two outstanding philosophers of the period, Kant and Hume, tussled with this problem. Lewis Beck, in his article on Kant and his educational thought, notes that Kant was one of the few philosophers to have both written on education and had actual experience as an educator. He recalls Kant's early years as a private tutor, his work as a propagandist and fund-raiser for the innovative Dessau Philanthropin and his forty-three-year career as a university professor. Reviewing the editorial history of Kant's lectures on pedagogy, Beck concludes that there is no reason to assume that this work is an authentically organized account of Kant's ideas on education, and suggests that the unifying thought in Kant's educational theory should be sought in his other writings.

Beck raises the problem of the seeming dichotomy in Kantian thought with respect to moral education. On the one hand, his strict moral philosophy precludes moral training, for, unlike Rousseau, Kant does not see morality as one of the natural dispositions of the child that can be brought to actualization by training. On the other hand, passages in his writings suggest that while an awareness of morality cannot be created by education, it can be made salient by the skilful teacher.

This is the problem to which Samuel Ajzenstat addresses

himself in his paper. Ajzenstat argues that, despite its chequered editorial history, Kant's *On Education* deserves serious consideration, not as a set of opinions in the theory of education detached from his general philosophical position, but as a book that "points directly to the most difficult problems in Kant." He sees in the work the same tension between means and ends that runs through much of the main body of Kantian philosophy. Morality and freedom, the goals of education, are based upon self-control which yields neither to external forces nor to internal feelings. Self-control, however, is to be taught by the external forces of reward and punishment and internal feelings of pleasure and pain. But if self-control is true *self* control and not control by some other, then moral education would seem to be a meaningless notion.

Not necessarily, Ajzenstat argues. A careful examination of Kant's basic philosophical position, he suggests, shows that the essential problem which he sets himself is to demonstrate that "human thought and action need not be impervious to the causal processes of nature in order to retain a rational ability to reach to the universally and necessarily valid, especially in the moral life; rather that natural processes of various kinds must be understood as working towards the end of producing a being with the capacity for rational self-determination." Thus, Ajzenstat concludes, *On Education* gives the educator the mandate to discipline the child with the assurance that such causal manipulations can be instruments in the services of rationally a priori self-determination.

Unlike Kant, David Hume wrote no specific treatise on education, but James Noxon demonstrates in his essay in this collection the importance of his contribution to eighteenth century educational theory should not be underestimated. The key to the seeming inharmony of Hume's remarks on education — that it is the principal source of false belief, and that it is indispensible to civilization — lies, Noxon argues, in the clear distinction which Hume makes between cultivating intellect and moulding character. In subjects of purely intellectual concern Hume maintains that pupils should be encouraged to test what they are taught about reality against their own experience, and should not be indoctrinated with beliefs that cannot be verified. In matters of morality, however, he holds that pupils should be trained, by indoctrination, to behave according to the conventions of the society for which they are being prepared. In his perceptive analysis of the philosopher's correspondence with two fathers of his acquaintance, Noxon suggests that Hume considered the moral and social development of the student to be of such importance that he was prepared to forgive intellectual weakness in teachers so long as they were earnest about the inculcation of virtue.

While the great thinkers of the age pondered the philosophy of education, an astonishing number of lesser known men and women expressed their concern with education on a more mundane level. In France, for example, nearly 200 books and pamphlets on education — written by everyone from prominent lawyers to military men, literary hacks, private tutors, and aristocratic fathers — were published between the death of Louis XIV and the outbreak of the Revolution. Conscious, to varying degrees, of contemporary theories of learning and affected by the century's new sensitivity to the child, these authors criticized the educational status quo and called for sweeping reforms.

One of the numerous issues they debated was whether a child should be educated at home or in a public institution. Locke, in his *Some Thoughts upon Education,* and Rousseau, in his *Emile,* both advocated that children be taught at home where parents could maintain closer supervision over them and where they would not be exposed to moral corruption by school fellows. Those who accepted this viewpoint were, for the most part, convinced that no one else would have the same degree of interest in the child as his own parents, or the same care for his moral welfare. Even those who opted for public schooling attached great importance to the involvement of parents in the upbringing of their children. It was not uncommon for authors to address their books, even ones dealing primarily with technical matters such as improved methods of teaching languages, to fathers on the assumption that they would, or should, be interested in these things. Mothers, too, were granted a recognized, if restricted, function in the educational process. In addition to the task of breastfeeding their infants and generally overseeing their early years, they were assigned special responsibility for forming their children's character.

But the overwhelming majority of French writers supported public rather than domestic education. They contended that children who were accustomed from an early age to get along with their fellows would be better prepared for their adult life as members of the community. Of course the quality of the schools was of crucial importance. One of the reformers' prime targets was teaching techniques, which they wanted modified to conform with current knowledge about the nature and limitations of children. Childhood, they insisted, should be a happy time. Youngsters should be encouraged to learn by gentle masters, rather than forced to study through fear of punishment. Since their intellects were less developed than those of adults, young pupils must not be expected to memorize vast quantities of material they could not possibly understand. Instead, teachers should arouse their natural curiosity and appeal to their senses, which were held to be especially acute at this age. Visual aids in the classroom, educational games that would amuse at the same time as they instructed, and short lessons interspersed with periods of recreation were among the methods they recommended for making learning a pleasant and effective experience.

What precisely should be taught in the schools was a matter of some controversy, however. Although there was almost unanimous agreement among educational writers that the existing curriculum needed to be reformed, when it came to making specific proposals about what should replace it they were often at odds. In part this was a result of the idiosyncracies and personal hobby-horses of the individual authors. But it was also a reflection of the range of different opinions they held about what the fundamental goals of the new curriculum should be.

It is possible to discern three major, though by no means mutually exclusive, forces motivating the critics' pleas for change. First, there was frustration with schools whose programs, devoted almost entirely to Latin, did not meet modern needs. Reformers whose primary aim was to provide students with a relevant, practical education demanded an updated syllabus that would teach history, geography, science, and modern languages. Second, there was worry about the moral well-being of the child. Complaints were widespread that the schools, through what was perceived as lax discipline and neglect of moral training, were contributing to the corruption of young people. Those whose main preoccupation was to form upright individuals called for special courses in ethics, a literary syllabus selected on the basis of its moral value, and history classes designed to demonstrate that, throughout the ages, virtue has been rewarded and wickedness punished. Finally, there was the conviction that the educational system should be oriented to the needs of the state. Writers who were determined to raise children committed to their country, as Leith's paper on the inculcation of national patriotism reveals, drew up their curriculum proposals with this goal in mind.

French books and pamphlets on education, Leith finds, reflected the growing sense of national consciousness in the country. Motivated by a desire to increase attachment to the state, many would-be reformers sought ways of inspiring patriotism in the child and of creating a uniformity of outlook throughout France. Leith describes the remarkable range of proposals which they presented. A number of writers advocated some sort of government agency to control and direct education. Some recommended instruction in civics, others the deliberate manipulation of subjects such as history and literature to encourage attachment to France. Stressing the importance of role models, the "multi-media men" proposed the glorification of national heroes, not only in prose, but in poetry, songs, and imagery as well. The Age of the Enlightenment, Leith reminds the reader, was not simply "an age when men threw off authority, when they affirmed their autonomy, [it] was . . . also an age when many educators advocated rigid state control, mass indoctrination and a homogenized citizenry."

The question remains, how much of this theory was actually put into practice? What impact did the new attitudes towards children and education have on the manner in which parents treated their offspring and on the ways in which the schools taught them? Lawrence Stone's pathfinding studies underline that there can be no simple answers to these questions. Society, he points out, far from being homogeneous, consists of a number of strata and subgroups, each of which has to be studied separately if any valid understanding of the response of an age to new ideas is to be achieved. It is here that the case study can contribute so effectively. Stone, for example, suggests that the English nobility on the whole responded favourably to the idea that children be educated at home. The exception was the high court aristocracy which continued to have little involvement with its children, generally abandoning them completely to the care of nurses, governesses, tutors and schoolmasters. One conclusion that might be drawn from Gregg's study of the education of Queen Anne and her royal contemporaries is that in its treatment of its offspring the higher aristocracy was perhaps modelling itself upon the behavior of the royal court itself.

Political concerns, Gregg argues in his essay, transcended all other considerations in the upbringing of royal children in the late seventeenth and early eighteenth centuries. Children were physically and emotionally isolated from their parents from birth and raised in separate establishments directed by governors and governesses. The consequences of this upbringing, he suggests, was that the young prince or princess frequently grew up to be a generally unsociable adult, with a strong desire for privacy. The system weakened (or destroyed) emotional ties between members of the royal family and, conversely, allowed members of the royal youngsters' households to develop an influence over their charges that might well survive into their later lives.

King delves into a very different social milieu in his examination of the early education of Pope. The poet's Roman Catholic teachers, King suggests, may have had more influence on him than has been suspected. Recreating Pope's early school years, King notes that his education at the hands of secular priests and laymen was typical of the evolution of Roman Catholic education of the period away from religious orders. The men under whom Pope studied were devoted Catholics who had suffered persecution for their beliefs. Challenging Pope's own assessment of his elementary education ("I never learned anything at the little schools"), King asks whether Pope, in fact, did not learn from his schoolmasters something very significant about the difficulties attendant upon being a Catholic in late seventeenth-century England.

Efforts to implement new educational ideas and to introduce revised school programs were bound to meet with resistance from the more traditional segments of society. Strangely, this problem of how the transition from old to new was to be accomplished was largely ignored by eighteenth-century commentators. Yet, short of a revolution that would forcibly sweep away the status quo, something not envisaged by the average writer, it was inevitable that the old and the new should exist side by side for a certain period of time. And it was equally inevitable that friction and tension would result.

To the twentieth-century observer it may well seem that the period of transition would be a lengthy one, with battle positions drawn ultimately along generational lines. If a new system of education based on Enlightenment principles and priorities were successfully introduced, it would produce a generation with a different set of values, almost a different culture, from their elders. The young people raised under the new order would, when they grew up, find themselves face to face with institutions and an Establishment created by the old. Changing the schools would therefore in turn require restructuring society as a whole, as the products of the enlightened schools set about making institutions around them conform to the values they had been taught. Consciously or unconsciously this was, of course, what most writers hoped for when they advocated educational reform. What they chose to ignore was the tension, conflicts and social confusion that the process would entail.

Greenbaum's paper on the Paris Hôtel-Dieu immediately prior to the French Revolution is a study in microcosm of the encounter of new educational ideas and practices with traditional values and procedures. Greenbaum analyzes the struggle for the mastery of the hospital which took place between the physicians and surgeons, champions of clinical medicine, and the nurses, upholders of the belief that the primary obligation of healing was to cure the soul. Triggered by first-surgeon Pierre Desault's inauguration within the hospital of a surgery school and clinic and by new regulations subordinating nurses to the direction of the staff doctors, the clash was a protracted and bitter one. Convinced of the justice of their position, neither side was willing, or able, to compromise. The outbreak of the French Revolution in 1789 found the conflict still unresolved.

Philosophy, proposals, practice and consequences: education in the eighteenth century, despite recent scholarly interest, remains, to a surprising degree, uncharted territory. The papers in this interdisciplinary collection make a welcome contribution to our understanding of a complex and fascinating field of inquiry.

Annette Bridgman

Kant on Education

Kant was one of the few philosophers who have both written on education and had actual experience as an educator, experience that was had by neither Locke nor Rousseau. Kant's experience as an educator can be summarized under four headings: his work as a house tutor, his work as a propagandist and money-raiser for the Dessau Philanthropin, his career as a university professor, and his lectures on pedagogy to university students.

From 1749 to 1754 (the dates are only approximate, but probably not wrong by more than a year) Kant was *Hauslehrer* in two or three families near Königsberg. From 1749 to 1750 or 1751 he instructed the children of Pastor Andersch in Judtschen, from 1751-1754 those of Major von Hülsen in Arnsdorf, and perhaps in 1754-55 those of Graf Keyserling in Rautenburg. We know little of these years, since there is only one letter extant that has any bearing on his tutorial duties, and it is only a brief letter of courtesy accompanying a gift of some books to the boys in the Hülsen family. Years later Kant said that "there probably never was a worse tutor than I"[1], but he must have been satisfactory, for later he was consulted by one of his former pupils about the appointment of a tutor to his children; and it is well known that he had long continued social relations with the von Keyserling family; the earliest portrait of Kant was painted by the Gräfin von Keyserling, and the Keyserling boys when they came to the University were placed in Kant's care. We do not know what benefits the children gained from Kant's lessons; we can be more confident that Kant learned much from the social intercourse he had with the noble families with which he lived. Kant had been brought up in very straitened financial circumstances and an inelegant social milieu; when he returned to Königsberg about 1755 he was apparently fluent in French, polished in the artificiality of aristocratic conversation, something of a dandy in dress and comportment, and the "galant master" as he was

---

1. H. Jachmann, *Immanuel Kant geschildert in Briefen an einen Freund*, Second letter, second paragraph.

known in the University. How good a tutor to the children Kant was I do not know, but he was an apt pupil of their parents.

Johann Bernard Basedow was deeply influenced by Rousseau but in personality as ill-adapted as Rousseau for the practical work of being a school administrator (Herder said of him that not only children, but cattle, should not be entrusted to his care[2]). Through his earlier writings and then through the curriculum he instituted Basedow attempted to realize Rousseau's teaching. Teaching was to be through dialogue and play; emphasis was to be displaced from exercising memory to exercising observation and thinking; French and Latin were to be taught by actual use in conversation; character development and mechanical skills were emphasized, and moral education was to be independent of religious instruction but the child was to be brought gradually to recognize the truths of natural religion. Each teacher was encouraged to experiment and to develop his own program and technique of teaching. Basedow's writings on educational reform, subsidized by enlightened despots like Joseph II of Austria and Catherine the Great of Russia, had attracted wide attention, and in 1774 with a grant from Prince Leopold of Dessau (to whom he had been introduced by Goethe) he established his school in Dessau. Two years later, in May 1776, there was a public exhibition through performances by the pupils and public examinations to which many of the leading people of Germany were invited, and attention to the school was attracted throughout Germany. Unfortunately there were more visitors than pupils, for Basedow had succeeded in getting only thirteen children, two of whom were his own. Basedow was removed and was followed by Wolke and Campe, who were more competent administrators.

Kant became an enthusiastic backer of the Philanthropin in 1776. Basedow published an account of his school addressed to parents who wished to send their children to it, and Kant reviewed it in the Königsberg newspaper March 28, 1776.[3] "To every community, to every citizen of the world", he wrote, "it is important to learn about a new institution whereby a wholly new order of human affairs is to be brought about which will produce

---

2. Geothe's sketch of Basedow's character (*Dichtung u. Wahrheit,* Book XIV) is unlikely to inspire more confidence in him.

3. *Aufsätze, das Philanthropin betreffend.* Akademie Ausg. II, 446-52.

a wide reform both in private and social life." To help the school Kant volunteered to receive subscriptions to later numbers of the *Philanthropinisches Archiv*. A year later he reviewed the second volume of the reports on the Philanthropin, saying that what is needed is not a gradual reform but a sudden revolution in education, and that for this is required "only one school based on the genuine method of education, guided by enlightened men who will show the learned world what they can do, and who will teach students to follow the same method later in their own schools."[4] Again he urged parents to subscribe by sending their money to him.

On the same day that the first of these reviews was published, Kant wrote to Wolke recommending George Motherby, the six-year old son of his friend Motherby, describing how perfectly the Philanthropin fitted the educational ideals he and the elder George Motherby held in common;[5] a short time later he wrote Basedow[6] saying that Motherby thought every day lost that his son was not in the Philanthropin, and was about to leave Königsberg to bring him to Dessau. In 1777 there were many letters concerning the business of raising money for the school, one of which[7] shows, in the words of Kant's biographer Vorländer[8] *beinahe jesuitische Schlauheit* in Kant's successful efforts to flatter an influential local minister (Crichton), who had been critical of the Philanthropin, into taking over the money-raising effort.

All of Kant's efforts except this last were in vain; the school recovered for a while under new management, but finally closed in 1794. Kant wrote of its demise:

People imagine, indeed, that experiments in education are unnecessary, and that we can judge by our reason whether anything is good or not. This is a great mistake, and experience teaches us that the results of an experiment are often entirely different from what we expected. Thus we see that, since we must be guided by experiments, no one

---

4. Ibid., 446, 448.
5. Kant to Wolke 28 March 1776.
6. Kant to Basedow, June 19, 1776.
7. Kant to Wilhelm Crichton, July 19, 1778.
8. Karl Vorländer, *Immanuel Kant, der Mann und das Werk*, I, 225.

generation can set forth a complete scheme of education. The only experimental school which had in a measure made a beginning to clear the way was the Dessau Institute. This must be said in its praise, in spite of the many mistakes with which we might reproach it — mistakes which attend all conclusions from experiments — namely, that still more experiments are required. This school was in a certain way the only one in which teachers were free to work out their own methods and plans, and in which teachers were in communication with each other and with all the learned men in Germany.[9]

Kant had more experience than any of us have had in the practice of education as a university teacher. For forty-three years, without a sabbatical break, he lectured and held exercises for his students (disputatoria and repetitoria) in an appalling variety of fields including logic, metaphysics, ethics, anthropology, physical geography, physics, natural theology, pedagogy, and fortification engineering. His normal teaching load was fourteen hours a week, and he began lecturing at 7 o'clock in the morning. His lectures were famous in the University, and even brought students from foreign countries to hear them. Johann Gottfried Herder, a student of his in 1762 who later became embittered against him, nevertheless vividly remembered the lectures he had heard:

> I have had the good fortune to know a philosopher. He was my teacher. In his prime he had the happy sprightliness of a youth; he continued to have it, I believe, even as a very old man. His broad forehead, built for thinking, was the seat of an imperturbable cheerfulness and joy. Speech, the richest in thought, flowed from his lips. Playfulness, wit, and humor were at his command. His lectures were the most entertaining talks. His mind, which examined Leibniz, Wolff, Baumgarten, Crusius, and Hume, and investigated the laws of nature of Newton, Kepler, and the physicists, comprehended equally the newest works of

9. *Education* (University of Michigan Press, 1960) pp. 22-23. All subsequent references in the text which cite only a page number are to this edition. For reasons that will become obvious, however, when I have occasion to refer to this book by title I shall call it by its more accurate name, *Pedagogy*.

Rousseau . . . and the latest discoveries in science. He weighed them all, and always came back to the unbiased knowledge of nature and to the moral worth of man. The history of men and peoples, natural history and science, mathematics and observation, were the sources from which he enlivened his lectures and conversation. He was indifferent to nothing worth knowing. No cabal, no sect, no prejudice, no desire for fame could ever tempt him in the slightest away from broadening and illuminating the truth. He incited and gently forced others to think for themselves; despotism was foreign to his mind. This man, who I name with the greatest gratitude and respect, was Immanuel Kant.[10]

I turn now to Kant's activities as a teacher of education. In English-speaking countries the normal source of information on Kant's views on education is a small book entitled *Education* published by the University of Michigan Press from an earlier and undated translation by Annette Churton. There is, in this miserable volume, no word of identification or explanation, no indication of its provenance. We are not told what it is a translation of, and the added notes are mostly uninstructive. The numbered paragraphs are rearranged, we are told; but we are not told from what they are rearranged. The book is an example of how translations ought not be made and published.

And when one overcomes his initial distaste for a cheap and tawdry piece of presswork and begins to read it, suspicions about its authenticity are aroused. Kant, who was usually meticulous about organization — some say he was overly meticulous, and object to his scholastic architectonic organization — is here presented as a writer either incapable of or careless about good organization. He gives incompatible definitions and classifications, and did not even succeed in making his chapter heads correspond to the contents. Another thing which puzzles the reader is the familiarity of much of the material. There are, to be sure, discussions which have no counterpart in the remainder of Kant's writings; these are usually either quaint or boring, such as discussions of whether children should be rocked

10. Quoted from my edition of Kant's *Prolegomena* (Liberal Arts Press, k95k), p. xxii.

in cradles, attended to when they cry, and given the first flow of mothers' milk. One is reminded of Dr. Johnson's angry impatience with Boswell when Boswell asked him what he would do if he were left alone with an infant; Kant discusses these questions *ex officio,* as it were, and without putting his old bachelor's heart into it. But aside from these passages, the rest of the book seems to be made up of paraphrases, quotations, and slight misquotations from Kant's other writings. What is even worse, many of the passages have obvious parallels in Rousseau's *Émile.*

Faced with this mess, the curious reader will soon throw aside this wretched little book and, with curses on the Press, on Miss Churton, and perhaps even on Kant himself, will turn to the Akademie edition of Kant's writings to find the original. This is in volume 9 of the Akademie under the title *Immanuel Kant über die Pädagogik,* edited by Friedrich Theodor Rink and first published in 1803. It is not divided into chapters, as the translation is, so that the disorganization of the text is somewhat obscured since, as I have said, Miss Churton's chapter headings do not correspond very closely to the contents of the chapters. Nor do we find the paragraphs numbered, nor the total number of paragraphs corresponding to the numbers given in the translation. We do find a foreword by Rink that was not translated and we turn hopefully to it for enlightenment on what kind of book it is we have.

Rink says that the required course in pedagogy at Königsberg was given in turn by several of the professors of philosophy, and that when it was Kant's turn (in 1776-1777, 1780, 1783-1784, and 1786-1787) he used as the basis for his lectures the *Textbook in the Art of Education* by his colleague Bock but "held himself exactly neither to the course of investigations nor to the principles" of that book. "To this circumstance", he says, "we owe the origin of the following remarks (Bemerkungen) on pedagogy".[11]

In the light of these introductory statements, it has been commonly believed that we have here a work comparable to the *Lectures on Ethics,* edited by Paul Menzer from a careful collation of several *Kolleghefte* by students in the class, or to the *Lectures on Logic* which Jäsche compiled by taking Kant's marginal notes in the Meier textbook upon which he lectured.

11. Ak. IX, 439.

This assumption has been refuted by an erudite, somewhat pedantic, and mammoth book by Traugott Weisskopf, *Immanuel Kant und die Pädagogik* (Basel, 1970). I can give only the highlights of this enormous commentary of over 700 pages on a text of sixty pages.

First, there is a question about Rink himself. The conclusions are that he was incompetent and dishonorable, and that the trust Kant had in him is to be explained only by reference to Kant's senility and to Rink's pretensions.

Second, the text is based neither on students' *Kolleghefte* nor on any lecture notes of Kant's, for there is no way even distantly to relate the contents either to Bock's text or to the text by Basedow which we know (though Rink does not mention it) was used as the textbook the first time Kant gave the series of lectures on pedagogy. Furthermore there is the reference to the demise of the Philanthropinum, quoted above, which occurred in 1794, years after the last lectures were given.

Third, the compiling done by Rink must have been simply the joining together of at least three piles of Kant's notes without any serious effort to avoid repetition or inconsistencies. These three conjectural and relatively independent collections were made by Kant at different times and for different purposes. (For convenience, I shall refer to chapter headings not present in Rink but introduced later by Miss Churton). Weisskopf identifies these sub-collections as: (a) lecture notes on *Anthropology*, used in the Introduction, chapters 4, 5, and part of 6; (b) a collection of quotations from Rousseau or notes on Rousseau which Kant apparently made from *Émile* in French and not from the German translation, used in chapter 3 and part of chapter 2; and (c) notes for Kant's *Lectures on Ethics*, used in chapter 6.

Weisskopf's fourth contention is that Rink added material of his own, as indicated by differences in style; and collation of Rink's transcriptions of passages we have in Kant's own *Nachlass* and in the published *Anthropology* and *Lectures on Ethics* shows that he modified Kant's own language when he was copying authentic sources.

Weisskopf's conclusion is that the text cannot be regarded as an authentic work of Kant's and should be removed from the corpus.[12] The documentation for the thesis is overwhelming, so

12. Weisskopf, p. 349.

much so that there is a high degree of pedantic overkill in Weisskopf's relentless prosecution of Rink. In my opinion Weisskopf has adequately supported his indictment. But I must confess to some doubt about his explanation of the way the Rousseau material got into the book. There are three considerations against it. First, from what we know of Kant's working methods, it seems very unlikely that he transcribed or translated, or even took such copious notes, as this hypothesis requires. Second, there is the absence from Kant's *Nachlass* of any of the notes; most of the Rousseau notes which have survived are included in the collection of material which was used in the sixties when he was working on or annotating the *Observations on the Feeling the Beautiful and the Sublime.* Third, and perhaps most important, is the fact that upon examination of each passage in Rousseau and Kant which Weisskopf sees as parallel, I do not find as many indisputable cases of parallelism as he does; and the differences between the German translation of *Émile* and the original, and the putative similarities of Kant's material to the latter and dissimilarities to the former seem to me to be, with perhaps one exception, so subtle and exiguous that I do not believe one can be confident that Kant was reading the original instead of a translation. But I must confess that I have no better explanation of the way the Rousseau material got into the Rink text, unless, of course, Rink put it there on his own authority.

It seems to me, however, that Weisskopf has proved too much for his own purpose. In fact, he has shown very good reason to take *Über die Pädagogik* seriously as a compendium of *echt-kantische* views on education, even if we cannot be confident that we are reading Kant's own words and can be generally confident that we are not reading them in an order and context established by Kant himself. Out of the 175 paragraphs of the German text (which do not correspond to the 113 numbered sections in the translation), Weisskopf has given at least conjectural documentation for all but thirty-one citations from other works of Kant, Kant fragments, the hypothetical collection of Rousseau notes, or Bock's textbook (which provides only a very small number). The thirty-one undocumented paragraphs contain no controversial surprises; they deal mostly with things which neither Kant nor the reader is very interested in. I come to the conclusion that though Weisskopf is on the whole correct in his scholarly and bibliographic research, though some of his parallel passages do not seem to me to be as parallel as they appear to him, the *Pädagogik* is still for the most part a compendium of Kant's views on education, disorganized, but inauthentic only in the cases where the text corresponds only in part to manuscripts in Kant's hand or to his other published works, and is interrupted by material not in extant manuscripts or published works and therefore presumably containing interpolations by Rink without Kant's authority. Accordingly, I think one should be warned against using any part of the text of Rink which has no counterpart in authentic Kant works or manuscripts, and when this correspondence *does* exist it is probably better to cite the sources which did not suffer mutilation at Rink's hands; this will be found possible in the case of the most important passages, and one should use other authentic works as a guide to and commentary on the Rink compilation.

While there is no objection to the cautious use of individual paragraphs in the Rink edition or even the Churton translation, especially if one has the Weisskopf at hand as a control, there is no reason to attempt to follow the work or the translation as a whole under the assumption that it presents an authentically organized account of Kant's thought on education. Accordingly, I shall find the unifying thought in Kant's educational theory not in the *Pedagogy* but elsewhere.

II

In the eighteenth century there was an intimate association of the philosophy of education with the philosophy of history. Lessing's most important work in the philosophy of history is entitled *The Education of the Human Race,* and Rousseau's educational doctrines cannot be understood without knowledge of the philosophy of history he had earlier expounded in the essays on progress in the arts and sciences and on the origin of inequality among men.

Kant's philosophy of history is a much more important base for his educational theory than his epistemology and *Anthropology* is. In the *Pedagogy* he raises the question: "Should we in the education of the individual imitate the course followed by the education of the human race through its successive generations?" (p. 12.). It is characteristic of the fragmentary character of this work that the question raised here is never explicitly answered in it. But if we turn to the papers on the philosophy of history we find that we have but little choice as to whether we shall interpret education as a recapitulation of history; the ages of an individual life correspond to the stages in the history of the world. By reading the fuller treatment of the philosophy of history we discover a key to the less well organized treatment of the philosophy of education.

On the *Conjectural Beginning of Human History,* which has some resemblance to the early parts of Lessing's *Education of the Human Race,* Kant interprets Genesis 2 - 6 as an account of the transition of man from a state of nature, guided by instinct, to a state in which he is guided, at first bunglingly, by the exercise of reason into the enjoyment and suffering of freedom. Prudence supervenes upon instinct, and man is able to foresee and prepare for the future. But the foresight into a future of the vanity of human wishes, labor, and death would have been sufficient to make man "foreswear and decry as a crime the use of reason, which had been the cause of all these ills" had it not been that "he came to understand, however obscurely, that he is the true end of nature, and that nothing can compete with him in this regard."[13] As the true end of nature, his own end must be one which is immune to the vicissitudes and constraints of nature: he is "released from the womb of nature" for a higher destiny in which he is an end in himself. Reason, produced by nature for the attainment of natural ends, creates ends of its own, and man makes the transition from civilization (a stage in the history of nature) to morality.

A like story, without biblical allegory, is told also in the *Idea for a Universal History.* Nature, he says, has willed that all the natural capacities of a creature are destined to evolve completely to their natural end and perfection, but this can be achieved only in the race, not in the individual. In this process, nature has ordained "that man should, by himself, produce everything that goes beyond the mechanical ordering of his existence, and that he should partake of no other happiness or perfection than that which he himself, independently of instinct, has created by his own reason."[14] Nature, using human vice and intelligence,

13. *Conjectural Beginning of Human History,* in *Kant on History,* ed. L.W. Beck (Bobbs Merrill, 1963) p. 58.

creates civilization, and could do so even with a race of devils, provided only they were intelligent devils. Morality is not a product of nature, but of a new beginning which, nevertheless, presupposes the natural processes leading up to civilization.[15]

With these keys, when we turn back to the *Pedagogy* we can see a pattern of organization which was formerly obscure. Kant divides education, like the history of the world, into three stages. He calls them nurture, discipline, and cultivation. (There are several other bipartite and tripartite divisions in the *Pedagogy*, and they are not all compatible with one another. The one I have chosen works as well as any of the others and is perhaps the one that is most perspicuous and pervasive.)

Nurture deals with the child purely as a part of nature. It is concerned with the feeding and tending of the young child. Kant acts like a Dr. Spock of the eighteenth century, and what he says (taken mostly from Rousseau) is of only antiquarian interest. I mention it only because this stage of education corresponds to the earliest stage in the history of the race, before the exercise of thought was possible or necessary and when all could be left to instinct.

The second stage of education, discipline, is that of the earliest school years. It is the discipline of mind and body under the general rubric of prudence (translated by Miss Churton as "discretion"). The teenage boy is no longer guided by mere nature, but by men who have themselves been educated; there is no *instinct* for education (pp. 6, 13). At this level the child is taught the proper use of his body and mind so that his "animal nature" does not get the better of his "manhood". Kant here speaks of learning games, reading, writing, music, swimming, obedience, and good manners, and of abilities which are valuable for achieving all sorts of ends. At this age the child is no longer like a dog or horse that must be "broken" (p. 20) but must be treated as a free being who has not yet developed full control of his own freedom.

The moral problem is how to unite submission to restraint with the child's capability of freedom; as Rousseau saw, restraint and freedom are antithetic, and yet the former is necessary to the latter. Kant states two principles to guide us through this difficult

14. *Idea for a Universal History, ibid.*, p. 13.
15. Ibid., p. 21.

period: We must allow the child every freedom which does not harm himself or others, and "we must prove to him that restraint is laid on him that he may learn in time to use his liberty aright, and that his mind is being cultivated so that one day he may be free, that is, independent of the help of others" (p. 28). Kant, unlike Rousseau, believes that public education, not education at home, is best for these purposes, since it teaches children how to get along with each other.

This second stage of education corresponds to the second stage in the history of mankind. In it, both the race and the child have left raw nature behind, but have not yet attained the level of morality. Historically, Kant calls this stage civilization; in it, outward decorum and the love of honor are a "simulacrum of morality", but civilization without morality is but "glittering misery".[16] (Almost exactly the same thing is repeated in *Pedagogy*, p. 21. Weisskopf (p. 560) finds three other almost identical passages in Kant's other works.[17])

The third stage of history and education is that of genuine morality. Because Kant makes so sharp a distinction between prudence, even at its highest and most disinterested level, and genuine morality, and because he is in no sense a "naturalist" in his ethical theory, the transition from the discipline of the natural talents and inclinations in civilized maturity to morality is especially difficult for him to deal with in theory, just as it is in fact difficult to manage in practice. Man is not moral by nature (108)[18], and morality is not one of the natural dispositions of the child that can be brought to actualization by training. Here he differs from Rousseau, who thinks the "germs" of morality are present from the beginning, as a natural disposition to the good. A moral disposition for Kant is a product of a "revolution in the heart".[19] A moral action is so free that it has no natural antecedents which produce it in the course of empirical, psychological development; a bad environment and evil companions are absolutely no excuse for immorality even though

16. Ibid., p. 21.
17. Weisskopf, p. 560.
18. *Anthropology from a Pragmatic Point of View*, transl. M.J. Gregor (Nijhoff, 1974), p. 185.
19. *Religion within the Limits of Reason Alone*, trans. H.H. Hudson and T.H. Greene (Harper, 1960), p. 36.

they may lead us confidently to expect it. The historical transition from a state of doctrinal religion (such as Kant finds in the Old Testament) to the state of moral religion (in the New) cannot, according to Kant, be explained historically;[20] it is as though a new revelation were responsible for it. Similarly the development of the individual's moral point of view from that of civility and decorum cannot be explained; we can at most, he says in the last sentence of the *Foundations of the Metaphysics of Morals,* explain its inexplicability, that is show that it is *not* an event occurring under the mechanism of nature.

The teacher, accordingly, cannot make the child moral; only the child himself can do that. Kant states that I have no duty even to try to bring another person to the state of moral perfection; another's moral perfection is not, like his happiness, one of the ends which it is a duty for me to try to achieve.[21] I have a duty to help the child perfect himself only in his *natural* abilities as a part of my duty to promote his happiness.

When Kant is dealing with education, however, he relaxes some of this rigor; he does not even seem to see that his strict moral philosophy has, and can have, no place for moral education. But in both the *Critique of Practical Reason* and the *Pedagogy* Kant seems to take it as self-evident that moral education is both obligatory and possible, and the only question about it is one of proper practice. Only in the *Lectures on Ethics* does he deal with the duty of education as such (including moral education) where he discusses it under the heading "duties arising from differences of age" as a sub-heading under "duties towards particular classes of human beings".[22]

In the *Lectures on Ethics* and in the *Pedagogy* he writes almost as if the *cultivation* of the moral disposition were like the *cultivation* of prudence, even though he still insists upon the great differences between morality and prudence. In the *Pedagogy* he writes: "Morality is something so sacred and sublime that we must not degrade it by placing it in the same

20. Ibid., p. 112.
21. *Doctrine of Virtue,* Part II of *Metaphysics of Morals,* trans. M.J. Gregor (Harper, 1964) pp. 44-50.
22. *Lectures on Ethics,* trans. L. Infield (Harper, 1963) pp. 247 ff. The point is well discussed by William Frankena, *Three Historical Philosophies of Education* (Scott Foresman, 1965) pp. 109-110.

rank as discipline" (p. 84), though discipline is (normally, at any rate) a precondition of morality:

"It cannot be denied that in order to bring either an as yet uneducated or degraded mind into the path of the morally good, some preparatory guidance is needed to attract it by a view to its own advantage or to frighten it by fear of harm. As soon as this machinery, the leading strings, have had some effect, the pure moral motive must be brought to mind."

When a person uncovers the moral law within,

"It gives his mind a power, unexpected even by himself, to pull himself loose from all sensuous attachments (so far as they fain would dominate him) and, in the independence of his intelligible nature and in the greatness of soul to which he sees himself called, to find himself richly compensated for the sacrifice he makes."[23]

The child can be brought to this awareness, Kant thinks, by telling him a story of innocence punished (his suggestion is that of Ann Boleyn!) and having the child recognize the difference between what prudence would dictate (agreement with the King in his false accusations) and what morality demands (let justice prevail though the heavens fall) and asking him, in his safety and innocence, which path he would prefer to follow (even though he admits he might not be courageous enough to do so). Through this story and this catechetical exercise, the child discovers within himself a disposition which Kant thinks does not come from nature, and cannot be created by education, but which can best be made salient by the skillful catechism of the teacher who helps the child draw the radical distinction between being prudent and being moral. In the *Metaphysics of Morals* (§52) he gives an example of such a moral catechism (not very realistic, we must admit) whereby a child is brought to see that morality is worthiness to be happy, and not happiness itself.

Kant's philosophy of history is, on the whole, a theodicy. He finds the meaning of history to lie in the dominance of morality over nature, and in the achievement of moral goals which he

23. *Critique of Practical Reason*, trans. L.W. Beck (Liberal Arts Press, 1956), p. 156.

believes are adumbrated in the course of history. Similarly he sees education as a means to enlightenment and eventually to a moral commonwealth, the church invisible or the Kingdom of God on earth. More modestly he writes: "Children ought to be educated not for the present, but for a possibly improved condition of man in the future; that is, in a manner which is adapted to the *idea of humanity* and the whole destiny of man" (p. 14). Education should be for this future, and this future can be attained only through education. "How then is this perfection [of humanity] to be sought? Wherein lies our hope? In education and in nothing else."[24]

Lewis Beck

24. *Lectures on Ethics*, p. 252.

Kant on Education
and the
Impotence of Reason

As a source of insight into Kant's philosophy the sixty pages that appear in the standard edition of his works under the title *Immanuel Kant über Pädagogik*[1] will not at first seem very promising. Erratically organized, at once incoherent and repetitious, frequently trivial and apparently self-contradictory, they may well baffle even the most teleologically-minded reader's efforts to see in them the hand of an ordering intelligence. Furthermore, it might seem plausible to argue that Kant's philosophical concern is with just those concepts and principles that are not produced in us by education, because no education, indeed no empirical consciousness, could occur unless we already possessed them; in that case his account of education, even if it were more lucid, would have to be seen as a matter of pragmatic side-issues incapable of adding anything to universal and necessary philosophical structures.

If this view of it were correct, *On Education* would not only be unable to contribute to essential Kantian doctrines; it would not be able to contradict them either. Consequently, when it is noted that the work contains passages that appear to conflict with what are taken to be Kantian fundamentals, it is tempting, especially in view of its chequered editorial history, to replace the charge of triviality with one of inauthenticity.

Charges of this kind are, in the nature of the case, hard to refute. However, if we simply drop them and try taking *On Education* seriously it becomes a much more interesting book,

---

1. *Akademie* edition, Vol. IX, pp. 437-499. The most readily available English translation of the work is Immanuel Kant, *Education*, trans. Annette Churton (Ann Arbor: Ann Arbor Paperbacks, University of Michigan Press, 1960). There is no date of translation in the Ann Arbor edition. However, another translation by E. F. Buchner, published in 1904, gives it as 1899. I have called the work *On Education* but have otherwise used the Churton translation. The references beginning with a "P" are to the numbered paragraphs or groups of paragraphs into which it is divided. For an account of the editorial history of this material see Lewis White Beck, this volume.

for it points directly to the most difficult problems in Kant and in doing so reminds us that we cannot take apparent Kantian "fundamentals" for granted. On the contrary, passages that seem to contradict them, even if they appear in a relatively minor, badly edited work, must be approached as an opportunity to revise our understanding of what our philosopher is about.

Thus the passages that make the work seem most dubious are precisely the ones that make it impossible to treat it as a set of opinions in the theory of education quite detached from Kant's general philosophical position. The discussions of education which enter into many of the most important of Kant's works we may at first use merely to supplement and provide independent confirmation of aspects of *On Education*; but they also serve to make it clear that Kant's interest in education is part of a broader set of concerns. And once we set out to integrate the fragmented notes that make up *On Education* into more finished Kantian structures we shall find that we have to produce an interpretation of the critical philosophy as a whole that allows education as Kant describes it to play a fundamental part.

The more clearly we can see its philosophical role, the easier it will be to explain some of the peculiarities of *On Education*. Thus considered merely from the educationist's point of view the book will surely appear much too narrowly focused on moral questions. Certainly it is single-mindedly concerned from beginning to end — even in those sections devoted to physical education — with the moral development of the child. But this is not because Kant failed to recognize other aspects of education; rather, as we shall see, it is because Kant's ethical theory raises questions that make moral education a central philosophical concern in a way that other aspects simply are not.

This point should not be misunderstood. There is a perfectly acceptable sense of the word "moral" according to which all education, insofar as it is felt to communicate worthwhile things, is moral education. But it is precisely this sense of the term that Kantian ethics regards as somewhat dubious. Thus, in spite of the celebrated tale that the only occasion on which Kant missed the daily walk by which his neighbours could count on setting their watches was on the day Rousseau's *Emile* arrived and in spite of the many echoes of the *Emile* in *On Education*, there is a crucial difference between these two works on moral education, a difference which can help us to see why *On Education* would have to have been one of Kant's minor works whereas *Emile* is Rousseau's masterpiece. Though there is undoubtedly much in Rousseau that prefigures Kantian ethics, there is also, in the *Emile* especially, a clear concern for the production of an integrated, happy person in whom the artifices of reason adapt themselves harmoniously to the natural necessities of desire. For Rousseau, at least part of the time, moral education has thus to concern itself with the entire range of human inclinations. Kant, however, devotes himself to the elaboration of a much more austere ethic, glimmerings of which he may have found in Rousseau, in which whatever is justified by natural desire alone is for that very reason not moral because not free and must consequently be held down and transcended. This is why, beside the *Emile* especially, *On Education* is likely to seem such a thin, dry treatise. That emphasis on natural feeling which gives the *Emile* so much of its richness is in Kant to a large extent what education must teach us to be able to cut away in order that we may claim our full moral patrimony. Without those incidental references elsewhere that link education to the larger structure of Kantian thought, *On Education* would be bound to seem a narrow and arbitrarily limited work, hardly worthy of serious attention.

Read outside of the larger context *On Education* will in fact often seem not so much a philosophical work as a sermon or series of newspaper editorials in which a crotchety old man trots out the grand old cliché that there can be no freedom without discipline. Near the beginning, for example — and the example could be multiplied — Kant tells us that children

> are first sent to school, not so much with the object of their learning something, but rather that they may become used to sitting still and doing exactly as they are told. And this to the end that in later life they should not wish to put actually and instantly into practice anything that strikes them. (P4)

Such a statement, I would venture to say, will not seem either profound, thoughtful, or particularly interesting. Read in a larger context, however, it is capable of giving us a very special insight not only into the deepest concerns of Kant's philosophy and of the Enlightenment period but into a fundamental dilemma of a world view which we have largely inherited from them.

As long as we stay on the level of cliché it is easy enough to summarize the main lines of *On Education*. "Our ultimate aim," Kant says (P94) "is the formation of character." Character is defined at one point as "the firm purpose to accomplish something and then also the actual accomplishing of it." (P94) "It consists," he says elsewhere (P78), "in readiness to act in accordance with 'maxims'." A maxim is not simply a rule, but as Kant puts it here, a subjective rule, a rule which I have adopted inwardly as a relatively permanent principle of action. Whereas purely natural objects display consistency of nature simply because unchanging laws of nature govern their motions, it is the special capacity of a human being to achieve consistency by organizing his life by adopting a purpose and sticking to it in a methodical and self-disciplined way. "Unmethodical men are not to be relied on; it is difficult to understand them, and to know how far we are to trust them." (P78) Character is not the whole of morality, since as Kant is fond of pointing out we find it difficult to withhold a certain grudging admiration from wicked men who exhibit persistency of purpose even though we then call it "obstinacy" rather than "character". (P94) Nevertheless, character is at least a necessary condition of morality. Morality and freedom are the highest human capacities and they thus represent the goals of education. Both are based on the capacity for firm, unyielding purpose, the human capacity for self-control. The fundamental task of education is thus the teaching of self-control.

Self-control develops in two stages: (1) external controls; (2) the internalization of these. The broadest of Kant's ways of dividing up the subject matter of educational theory is between physical and moral education and it helps to solve some puzzles of interpretation if we can identify physical education with external controls and moral education — taking "moral" in the very broad way in which it is sometimes used — as internal control. On this interpretation we can, for example, understand why Kant says that we may "call the cultivation of the mind physical, in a certain sense, just as well as the cultivation of the body." (P63) And we may also see why he discusses the formation of character both in the physical and in the moral part of the book. External control is a prior condition of self-control.

Since the man of character is, as much as is humanly possible, one who will not be turned aside from his resolves, we must learn "to put our passions on one side. We must take care that our desires and inclinations do not become passions, by learning to go without those things that are denied to us." (P93) Furthermore, children "ought to be prevented from contracting the habit of a sentimental maudlin sympathy." (P93) Thus if we look at what Kant has to say even about the early days of infancy we find that most of his remarks come under two basic concerns: the avoidance of overstimulation which arouses appetites and passions, especially with regard to questions of feeding; (P38, 44 etc.) and what Kant calls "hardening the child" in the interest of which he approves of "a cool, hard bed," cold baths and work and disapproves of swathing, leading strings and stays. (P38-46).

As we might expect, the discussions both of obedience and punishment follow the general lines of the external-internal distinction. Thus the stage of absolute obedience seems to have as its appropriate correlate physical punishment, whereas voluntary obedience links up easily with moral punishment.

Though far from a detailed summary of this short work, the account I have given of it so far ought to be enough to communicate its basic argument and overall flavour. Quite apart from one's acceptance or rejection of the position stated in *On Education*, one is bound to be perplexed by a major tension in the argument which, if pressed, leads into the heart of some of the most difficult and intriguing problems of Kant-interpretation and of philosophy generally.

A graphic recent illustration of the problem appeared a few years ago in a newspaper story. According to this account a team of educational sociologists set up an experiment to test the intellectual motivations and attitudes of underprivileged children. Upon successful completion of each of a series of problem-solving tasks each child was to be paid a certain sum of money. Once the children were well into the swing of things the monetary reward was to be discontinued and the series carried on on the basis of whatever degree of sheer intellectual curiosity the rewarded tests had managed to elicit. The conclusion reported was that the attitude of underprivileged children to intellectual pursuits was unfortunately almost entirely — mercenary! Here we have a classic even if farcical case of a conflict between the medium and the message. Yet it is surely the case that an enormous amount of our ordinary educational practice is based on the belief that a student who performs a task long enough for the sake of a tangible reward will finally come to perform it for its own sake. Nor is it easy to be certain that this belief is false, even after it has produced the predictably Pavlovian result of generations of students whose mouths water when the bell rings. Yet there is a real tension here between means and ends.

A similar tension runs through *On Education* and, as we shall see, in a profounder form, through much of the main body of Kantian philosophy. If it is a mistake, however, it is not, I shall try to show, merely a silly mistake, but rather the only available solution to a philosophical problem that the Enlightenment to a large extent set for itself and therefore, the mistake that destroys the Enlightenment and with it a considerable part of modern philosophy. If it is a mistake.

In *On Education* the tension between means and ends takes the following form. Character is to consist of unswerving mental self-determination whose devotion to pure principle yields neither to external forces nor to internal feelings. Yet this character is produced precisely through the action of the external forces of reward and punishment on the internal feelings of pleasure and pain. To even the amateur psychoanalyst it must seem only too obvious that far from being a self-motivated moralist, Kant's man of character is merely the authoritarian personality dominated not by himself but by the super-ego he imbibed with his teutonic toilet-training. To argue in this way, however, is to beg precisely the question at issue, which is Kant's claim that early discipline produces effects that transcend the coercive means used to produce them. We must see what leads him to make this claim.

Before we do so, however, we must see the claim in the more radical form in which Kant makes it in his major works and to which there are references also in *On Education*. After all, what we have so far is very general indeed. There is hardly any ethical philosophy that does not require some form of self-control. Any purely naturalist ethics — egoism, hedonism, utilitarianism, for example — is likely to require me to refrain from implementing immediate desires in the pursuit of some more long-term goal and for such a theory the claim that self-control is learned through experience of pleasure and pain, far from being a source of tension, is positive confirmation.

What Kant means by self-direction or self-control is quite different, as a brief review of some of the fundamental doctrines of the critical philosophy may be sufficient to show. Newtonian physics and his own vindication of its deterministic structure in the *Critique of Pure Reason*, force (and allow) Kant to draw a sharp distinction between nature and freedom. Nature is a spatio-temporal succession of events thoroughly linked together in accordance with laws of cause and effect. Of Kant's complex argument for the validity of this view of nature only one aspect need be noted for present purposes — the connection between the causal integrity of nature and its experienceability. It is whatever we treat as an empirical property or manifestation of a substance or object that we must treat deterministically. This condition, furthermore, applies as much to empirically determinable human characteristics and behaviours as to any other properties or events. At the same time, however, Kant argues in his works on ethics, that a moral act must be thought of as free. The basic causal mechanism of observable human actions is inclination — that is, desire for pleasure. But a moral act, according to Kant, could not be characterized as one that I perform simply because I feel an inclination to do so. The idea of morality is the idea of an obligation to act in certain ways regardless of what I feel inclined to do. It is the idea of an unconditional obligation, or in the more familiar phrase, a categorical imperative. And Kant claims that human beings are able by rational thought to discover such unconditional obligations and act on them on no other grounds than the rational recognition of their unconditional force. In particular, such acts cannot be motivated by any psychological causation that can be empirically discovered to be active in me. Moral reason is thus identical with free will and in the recognition of duty I recognize myself as a being that transcends nature. It would seem, however, that insofar as this free, rational self stands above nature it must be totally impervious to any sort of natural causality. Kant's own words often suggest that reason is a self-generating or self-actualizing power. And from this he appears to draw the conclusion, as one commentator puts it, that "to act freely is, at any time, in each rational man's power; hence every rational man is, at all times, responsible."

We are thus left with a strange image of two radically different selves somehow co-existing in one person, one of them observable and a product of empirical causation, the other free and presumably unobservable; one of them required by the causal integrity of nature in the light of the new physics, the other required to guarantee that the new physics will not undermine the moral and spiritual capabilities of man.

Returning now to *On Education* we find that the account just given seems to be grossly incompatible with what Kant says there about the moral development of the child. The problem is well put, for example, though not solved, by William Frankena:

> What Kant says makes it look as if he thinks that the whole temporal process which we call moral development, struggle, etc., is merely the appearance in space and time of a non-temporal act of choice made by one's real self. This seems to imply that moral education is not just phenomenal, but epiphenomenal, a kind of lantern-show reflecting what is really going on behind the scenes. We may have to engage in it but the issue is decided elsewhere.[2]

Frankena here brings to bear Kant's distinction between phenomenon and noumenon in the way that Kant is generally taken to have used it to allow for the compatibility of the two radically different accounts of self. Kant is interpreted as saying that the familiar self of ordinary experience, the self to which we apply empirical cause-effect analyses, is a mere phenomenon or appearance. Since Kant's previous argument has justified the causal principle only as a condition of experienceability and not as a generally valid metaphysical condition of being as such, he can leave open the possibility of the non-experienceable but nevertheless thinkable — the noumenon — which, since it need not meet the conditions of experienceability need not be the effect of a temporally prior cause within the unity of time.

The result of such a "two-tiered" account of self seems to be, as Frankena indicates, to make moral education a meaningless notion. In particular it would seem incapable of being the source of that peculiarly Kantian self-control for which Kant appears nevertheless to have designed it. For Kant self-control has moral significance only when it is truly *self*-control, not, at bottom, control by some other; for it to be possible requires that there be a radically self-determining stratum of self, independent of

2. William K. Frankena, *Three Historical Philosophies of Education* (Glenview: Scott, Foresman, 1965), p. 130.

external causality — educational or otherwise. Kant identifies this stratum with moral reason and argues that it is capable of recognizing the status of principles of action which are logically self-justifying and therefore proper to a self-determining being. The idea of such a self hardly seems to sit well with the idea of moral education or with the idea that its own coming-to-be is any process of causal development.

But it is just this appearance of incompatibility between Kant's views on education and the more or less received account of his thought that gives these views their special value. On the one hand, if we take them seriously they encourage us to attempt to formulate an interpretation of Kant's theory of self in line with them; on the other hand, everything that makes them hard to take seriously — their editorial sloppiness, for example — sends us to look for hints of a similar doctrine in the more reputable works, where it turns out to be easy to find. Here, however, I wish for the most part to short-circuit the larger project by taking *On Education* seriously, roughing out the interpretive possibilities it suggests and surveying, in a tentative way, some implications.

It is true that Kant himself often seems to express misgivings about the idea of a causal development or evolution of morality. Even in *On Education* he says (P78), "Morality is something so sacred and sublime that we must not degrade it by placing it in the same rank as discipline." But two pages later we find the following:

[Punishment] is moral when we do something derogatory to the child's longing to be honoured and loved (a longing which is an aid to moral training); for instance when we humiliate the child by treating him coldly and distantly . . . Hence this kind of punishment is the best, since it is an aid to moral training — for instance, if a child tells a lie, a look of contempt is punishment enough, and punishment of a most appropriate kind. (P83)

And two pages after that:
It is vain to speak to children of duty. They look upon it in the end as something which if not fulfilled will be followed by the rod. (P86)

These statements and others like them that we have glanced

at take us far from the exalted conception of the free and responsible moral agent. We might try to get around them and the entire document in which they appear by seeing Kant as trying to cope with the obvious fact that we are not born with a sense of moral responsibility. We could then argue that, like any "innate-idea" philosopher, Kant is forced to show more or less transcendent potentialities being actualized as they are given experiences to work on as the child grows towards eventual responsibility.

The moral actualization model, suggesting, as it does that education is a merely necessary, not a sufficient, condition of moral actualization because its function is to awaken a transcendent potentiality that is already there, seems like a more modest imposition of nature on freedom than a thoroughgoing determinism would be. In fact it raises equally difficult barriers against the idea of a universal human moral responsibility. Certainly *On Education* contains passages easily read in the light of the model as suggesting that education merely leads the child to the brink of a moral breakthrough which he then accomplishes "all by himself." Among these, for example, are those that contrast morality and discipline and exalt the former over the latter as well as those that argue that subtler teaching methods, using historical and literary "role-models" should be added to punishment and reward. But it will not help to read Kant's theory in this way: the problem remains how we can legitimately hold someone responsible and attribute moral freedom to him when the emergence or non-emergence of his moral consciousness depends on whether the necessary external conditions are present. One does not neutralize the role of education simply by downgrading it to a "merely necessary condition". Responsibility will not materialize if its merely necessary conditions are absent. Simply as a statement about children this might be of limited philosophical importance (though I doubt it). But clearly whole generations or nations might fail to receive the proper education with presumably rather momentous politico-moral consequences. Insofar as the laws of a nation can easily be seen as having an educational function on Kant's account of education it follows that

A good constitution is not to be expected from morality but

conversely a good moral condition of a people is to be expected only under a good constitution.[3]

Kant would seem to be suggesting, after all, that to act freely is not, at any time, in each rational man's power; hence that every man is not, at all times, responsible. Even as a merely necessary condition of moral development, the idea of education seems effectively to undermine the idea of conditional responsibility which Kant is usually thought to have put forth. And it is not too far-fetched to suggest that once unconditional responsibility goes so does any responsibility. Furthermore, as we shall see, these considerations raise serious questions as to the role to be assigned to the noumenal self in the context of an educational system that makes even a partial use of psychological cause-effect manipulation.

All of this might make it seem plausible to suggest that Kant changed his mind rather drastically at some point, giving up, perhaps gradually, the idea of morality as the work of a transcendent spiritual agency, impervious to natural causality, and replacing it with a more relativized conception of a self whose ability either to recognize duty (i.e., to recognize his own rational nature) or to act on it requires not merely the conceptual Kingdom of Ends but a flesh-and-blood supportive (and coercive) community. The ultimate implication of such a change would be that morality and reason as such are historical products, so that man cannot claim a prior validity for any moral principle.

Among the good reasons for avoiding the suggestion of such a drastic change of mind in Kant I shall mention only one. Almost all the works of Kant's philosophical maturity contain *both* the claim that human reason has universally and necessarily valid features *and* the claim that human reason undergoes a historical development which is of the nature of an education. What is wrong with the suggestion of a drastic change of mind is, in short, that it is based on the erroneous view that Kant in his greatest moral works saw his theory as requiring a self that was causally impervious as a guarantee of rational autonomy. To take this view is to assimilate Kant's philosophy in a fundamental

---

3. Immanuel Kant, *On History*, ed. Lewis White Beck (Indianapolis: Bobbs-Merrill, 1963), pp. 112-13.

way to that of Descartes and to miss a basic feature of Enlightenment thought as it presents itself in Kant.

Commentators have often written as if Kant's basic philosophical position was, in spite of important modifications, essentially the same as Descartes' — that both, in order to guarantee the universal and necessary validity of knowledge found it necessary to see it as having its source in a spiritual self possessing its ideas innately, isolated from whatever was considered to be the world of causation, hence, impervious to natural change. It is in the light of this Cartesian view that Kant's description of the noumenal self is often read; it is in this light also that his views on education seem like a betrayal to an alien perspective. But, though Kant may occasionally revert to a quasi-Cartesian conception of self, the essential problem he sets himself is far different. It is to show that human thought and action need not be impervious to the causal processes of nature in order to retain a rational ability to reach to the universally and necessarily valid, especially in the moral life; rather, that natural processes of various kinds must be understood as working towards the end of producing a being with the capacity for rational self-determination. This is, of course, the culminating project of the *Critique of Judgment*; yet that work may also be misunderstood or regarded as a speculative grab-bag if it is not understood that the rest of Kant's philosophy requires that capacities for the a priori have their causal source in empirical processes and be viewed as the capacities of observable and hence causally determined beings.

To demonstrate adequately that Kant's major project consists of arguing that the a priori is a product of natural causal processes and that in this sense, the phenomenal self — in reference though not in meaning — *is* the noumenal self would require the pursuit of the implications of *On Education* far beyond the range of a short paper, requiring as it would a re-examination of the entire Kantian corpus. But it is possible to suggest even if merely programmatically and very inadequately the basic terms of such re-examination. This involves some account of the relation of empirical psychology and transcendental logic and of the meaning of the noumenon within that relation.

The conventional view of Kant as concerned to reconcile empiricism and rationalism ignores certain features common to

Kant's empiricist and rationalist predecessors that he regards as erroneous. The common feature relevant here is a form of argument that draws conclusions concerning the rational validity or invalidity of certain beliefs from an account of how human beings come to possess these beliefs. Thus we find in Descartes the dubious argument to the effect that certain ideas can be shown to be logically valid by being shown to have been given to us by a good God. This in turn is linked to the argument that thinking substance is an effect of spiritual causality only and is isolated from the system of extended beings and impervious to the causation of nature. Only if Kant had accepted something like this account of how we know that our a priori principles are correct would he need to identify the noumenal self as insulated against phenomenal causality; and he sometimes does seem to be going in this direction. But it can be argued that he does so only because of misgivings as to his basic project. For in the *Critique of Pure Reason* he draws an important distinction between the legitimacy of a concept, which is to be determined by a certain kind of logical investigation, and that concept's "*de facto* mode of origination", which is said to be the concern of a kind of empirical psychology.[4] Though a number of problems complicate the passage, it may plausibly be read as suggesting that a concept which is universally and necessarily valid, hence, *logically* non-empirical, in the sense that it does not derive its validity from empirical evidence, will nevertheless be *psychologically* empirical in its *de facto* mode of origination. This means, among other things, that knowing a certain principle to be a necessarily true foundation of all knowledge does not determine as non-empirical the processes by which I come to have it, though it might spur me on to some teleological speculations about how lucky I am to have come to have it as well as to the rejection of those empirical psychologies which could not give a causal account of my possession of such concepts. But on this view Kant would not need to reject an empirical psychology that identified a priori principles as, for example, neurologically innate. Such a causal theory would not, of course, establish validity, but on Kant's view it is not the business of psychology — empirical or rational — to concern itself with validity.

4. A84 B117-A87 B119.

If we now recall that the essential evidence that I have free will and hence, that I am a noumenon, is, according to Kant, that I am capable of discovering by thought and acting on principles which are unconditionally obligatory because they do not depend for their validity on anything I happen to feel inclined to do, it becomes possible to argue that the attribution of free will to an agent is the attribution of a certain logical status to the ideas for the sake of which he acts and therefore that it tells us nothing either about the de facto mode of origination of those ideas or about what causal processes lead him to act on his consciousness of their validity (i.e., for the sake of them). One's progress, perhaps endless, in becoming a noumenon can thus safely be said in an ultimate sense to be the work of nature.

Education, however, is not for Kant directly the work of nature as such. Thus, having said that "man can only become man by education. He is merely what education makes of him" (P7) he adds:

It is noticeable that man is only educated by man — that is, by men who have themselves been educated. Hence with some people it is want of discipline and instruction on their own part, which makes them in turn unfit educators of their pupils.

The little book *On Education* in other words forms an incomplete theoretical statement in that it takes for granted the existence of the educator.[5] It gives the already moralized parent or teacher the mandate to discipline the child with the assurance that such causal manipulations as we have described can be instruments in the service of rationally a priori self-determination. But in so doing it directs us to the question of who educates the educator. And insofar as it also acknowledges that proper education will take place in the context of perhaps considerable improper education because of the lack of discipline in some of the teachers, it raises the question of whether we may hope that moral enlightenment, either through education or otherwise, is a cumulative process. The first of these questions directs us to the past, the second to the future. Together they form the basis of Kant's attempts to construct a

5. As does the *Emile*.

philosophy of history on the casually naturalistic lines so far described. Some account of the relation of education and history may therefore form an appropriate conclusion to these remarks.

The education of the amoral by the amoral can be understood causally but seems to make no sense morally. The education of the moral by the moral makes moral sense but, because it takes the existence of the moral educator for granted is not by itself fully understandable causally. Turning first to the latter problem we find Kant suggesting in the Introduction to *On Education* that the question: how did these people come to be good? can be answered only by a regress through the generations to a point where we can see reason either emerging from nature or established in a radically non-natural way:

> One generation educates the next. The first beginnings of this process of educating may be looked for either in a rude and unformed, or in a fully developed condition of man. If we assume the latter to have come first, man must at all events afterwards have degenerated and lapsed into barbarism. (P3)

The reference to "a fully developed condition of man" as having "come first" seems to me most plausibly interpreted as Kant's concession to the Biblical account of creation according to which human reason undergoes no radically fundamental growth because humanity always was essentially what it is now. Insofar as this account squares with the Cartesian tradition of reason as non-naturally innate, Kant may very well have been reluctant to set it aside as a possibility; we need not see it simply as a prudential deferring to official religious prejudice. Nevertheless, even here, Kant takes the view that either way we must be ready to trace a development from "barbarism" to reason — a view that in effect undermines the explanatory force of an appeal to the creation of spirit alongside of nature. When we turn to that part of Kant's philosophy of history in which he makes the regress to origins we find a more overt undermining of the Biblical account, for a description of a naturalistic transition from instinct to reason or from animality to humanity is there presented precisely as an exegesis of the story of Adam and Eve in the Garden of Eden.[6]

This transition is precisely the transition which in *On Education* he argues must be repeated in every generation insofar as there is to be such a thing as moral education. The painful civilizing process which over a very long period of time produced what the third Critique calls "freedom of discipline" is speeded up in the educational process by more systematically and artificially imposed discipline but the goal is the same for "it is discipline which prevents man from being turned aside by his animal impulses from humanity, his appointed end . . . Discipline changes animal nature into human nature. (P 3, 4)

It must be remembered, however, that for Kant an account of origins answers only causal questions and not questions of validity which must be discussed in a logical and not a genetic framework. But, as I have suggested, Kant was at times uneasy about the naturalistic account and there is at least one passage in *On Education* which pinpoints that aspect of the theory that might very well arouse misgivings. Describing the aims of moral education early in the text Kant says:

It is not enough that a man shall be fitted for any end, but his disposition must be so trained that he shall choose none but good ends. (P18).

Moral man is free and responsible just because reason rules in him so firmly that he cannot act except on those principles he is aware are ratified by it. The implications of this view are not only that in one sense at least the good man is neither free nor responsible for his goodness but that the evil man is neither free nor responsible for his evil in any sense of those terms. And, whether or not with good reason, Kant seems sometimes to have found these implications unpalatable. Here, however, we can pursue this issue no further.

Similar problems are also the source of some ambiguity when we turn to the question of a moral interpretation of the amoral educator passing amoral principles on to the next generation. Whatever happened to our ancestors in the Garden of Eden and after, the result was, as we may say, that only some are free. But if, in beings biologically able to think, freedom and reason have their causal origin in the processes of natural psychological determinism is it not sensible to think that such processes are still at work and that their continual working may eventually bring all men to rational freedom as a result of in-

6. "Conjectural Beginning of Human History", trans. Emil L. Fackenheim in *On History* pp. 53-68.

stitutions of discipline which nature forces amoral men to set up for the realization of amoral purposes? In a striking statement from *Perpetual Peace*, part of which I have already quoted, Kant anticipates just such a cunning of history:

> many say a republic would have to be a nation of angels, because men with their selfish inclinations are not capable of a constitution of such sublime form. But precisely with these inclinations nature comes to the aid of the general will established on reason, which is revered even though impotent in practice . . . A good constitution is not to be expected from morality but conversely a good moral condition of a people is to be expected only under a good constitution . . . This, then, is the truth of the matter: Nature inexorably wills that the right should finally triumph. What we neglect to do comes about by itself, though with great inconveniences to us.[7]

The mechanics by which all this is expected to come about Kant indicates elsewhere[8] are that the selfish inclinations of men gradually produce the mutually limiting (hence disciplinary) political freedoms of a typically liberal constitution which in turn is supposed to produce a better atmosphere for moral development.

In *On Education* Kant distinguishes educational principles as they ought to be and as they generally are:

> children ought to be educated, not for the present, but for a possibly improved condition of man in the future; that is, in a manner which is adapted to the *idea of humanity* and the whole destiny of man. (P15)

But:

> Parents usually educate their children merely in such a manner that, however bad the world may be, they may adapt themselves to its present conditions.

---

7. *On History*, pp. 112-13.

8. "Idea for a Universal History from a Cosmopolitan Point of View", trans. Lewis White Beck in *On History*, pp. 11-26.

Kant then adds the following sentence:

But they ought to give them an education so much better than this, that a better condition of things may be brought about in the future.

Read in the light of the passage from *Perpetual Peace* this is a perplexing sentence. According to that passage the grand moral future does not in the least depend on moral education in the present. We may even suspect that the selfish inclinations so heavily outweigh the moral will in leading the right finally to triumph — at least on Kant's rather dubious account of it — that a parent who gives a child a moral education is more likely to be unfitting the child to make any contribution to those political events, let alone survive.

Perhaps not much ought to be made of this difficulty. It is possible that Kant could be shown to regard the virtuous man and the immoral man as each making his distinctive contribution to a better future independently of the other. But we may still wonder why Kant regarded it as so important to be able to guarantee a better moral future deterministically that he was willing to mobilize the forces of evil in the march towards it.

What appears to worry Kant is that the more the virtuous man is concerned to change the present the more he will be tempted to adopt evil means. To be in a position to educate on a grand scale we must have political power and Kant, especially after the French Revolution, but before it as well, is painfully aware of the moral price to be paid for power. Because virtue requires that we evaluate our actions not as means to ends but as ends in themselves, the virtuous man ought not to pay that price. Will he be able to resist the temptation? Kant's answer in *On Education* is based on an optimistic account of human nature and educability:

the rudiments of evil are not to be found in the natural disposition of man. Evil is only the result of nature not being brought under control. In man there are only germs of good. (P16)

Elsewhere, however, Kant presents a much darker picture of radical human evil.[9] In the context of that darker picture it is not enough to warn man not to choose evil means to good ends. The very desire for a just world will be a source of corruption. What will ultimately keep even a virtuous man from backsliding into utilitarianism is, therefore, the doctrine that a virtuous man can safely leave the future that he craves in the hands of evil men for only they can bring it about and they must inevitably do so. Moral freedom and responsibility is thus tragically linked to political bondage and irresponsibility. To awaken in our children a sense of the power of reason within them we must teach them the historical lesson that it is "impotent in practice."

Samuel Ajzenstat

9. Immanuel Kant, *Religion Within the Limits of Reason Alone*, trans. Theodore M. Greene and Hoyt H. Hudson (2nd ed.; New York: Harper Torchbooks, Harper & Row, 1960).

Hume's Philosophy of Education

Schools played a minor role in David Hume's career, and he wrote neither treatise nor essay on education. He was registered at Edinburgh University on February 27, 1723, two months before his twelfth birthday. He left after three or four years without taking a degree. His biographer, E.C. Mossner, thinks it likely that he was prepared for the university at home in Ninewells by visiting tutors.[1] If so, Hume experienced no more than four years of institutional study, completing his formal education when he was about fifteen. Unlike most philosophers from Plato onward who have concerned themselves with principles of education, Hume was never a teacher. (I am disregarding his one year appointment as tutor to the Marquess of Annandale, since his solitary pupil was an unteachable lunatic.) Hume failed in his two attempts to secure professorships, first at Edinburgh, then at Glasgow, because of his reputation as a religious sceptic. Given the slightness of Hume's personal involvement in formal education, and the absence from his collected works of any systematic treatment of the subject, what did he contribute to eighteenth-century theory of education?

The answer, of course, is that Hume supplied a theory of learning. Epistemology is the foundational science of Hume's philosophical system. It is the basis upon which his emotive psychology, ethics, politics, aesthetics, his philosophy of history and of religion all rest. And it *is* the fundamental discipline out of which sound educational theory must be generated. Without elaborating a philosophy of education, Hume provided it with a basis which is in principle of the right sort, whatever its limitations and defects in detail. To many problems of educational theory currently discussed, a Humean solution could be extracted from his general theory of knowledge. And much of what his theory permits would sound strikingly modern. For example, his view of how habits of expectation are conditioned by experience could be made acceptable to operant behaviourists simply by translating his mentalistic terms into physicalistic ones.

1. *The Life of David Hume* (Oxford, Clarendon Press, 1954), p. 31.

Again, his evolutionary conception of primary thought processes as biologically determined means of adaptation would be congenial to Piaget's genetic epistemology. Such anticipations of contemporary learning theories latent in Hume's work would make convenient starting points for a modern history of educational philosophy.

What I am going to do, however, is to consider Hume's remarks on education in the light of his general philosophy. When he speaks as an epistemologist, he denigrates education as the principal source of false belief. When he speaks as a moral philosopher, he commends it as indispensible to civilized society. Since Hume did not suppose, as Mandeville did, that society is preserved by false beliefs, his two views of education appear inharmonious. My task will be to show that they can be reconciled.

I

Hume's epistemology, or "Logic", as he called it, was first set out in Book I of his first and greatest work, *A Treatise of Human Nature* (1739-40),[2] written in France when he was in his early twenties. A shorter and simpler version appeared nine years later under the title, *An Enquiry Concerning Human Understanding* (1748).[3] What is now called Hume's theory of knowledge is actually a theory of belief. For "knowledge", strictly defined, entails certainty, and it is Hume's chief and most original point that empirical judgements never have the certainty which deductive reasoning confers upon the conclusions of pure mathematics.

What we learn about the world through experience are matters of belief, therefore, and it is Hume's first intention to explain what psychological mechanisms operate when we acquire these factual beliefs. Although all our natural beliefs are grounded in sense experience and memory, according to Hume, belief in "such existences, as by their removal in time and place, lie beyond the reach of the senses and memory" (T 108) results from the inductive generalizations and inferences which habits of

---

2. Ed. L.A. Selby-Bigge (Oxford, Clarendon Press, 1888); abbreviated as "T" in parenthetical page references following quotations.

3. Ed. L.A. Selby-Bigge (Oxford, Clarendon Press, 2nd ed. 1902); abbreviated as 'E' in parenthetical page references following quotations.

association spontaneously generate. From the feel of the wind and the look of the sky, the sailor anticipates a storm. In his experience, similar conditions have invariably preceded rough weather. From the tracks in the snow, the deer hunter infers a running herd. He has learned to associate these visible effects with that kind of cause. The ideas of the storm and of the herd constitute natural beliefs. Both carry the same conviction as the sense impressions which evoked them through force of association.

When Hume calls those beliefs which are derived from everyday experience "natural", he means not only to describe, but also to commend them. He means not only that they result from laws of association at work upon the materials of accumulated experience but also that they are privileged. There is nothing feigned nor forced about them. They arise spontaneously and carry full conviction. They determine expectations, guide decisions, direct actions. They adapt human behaviour to the exigencies of nature.

Reasonable beliefs are those which conform to what is actually the case in the world, to what really happens. If predictions fail or projects go awry, we adjust our beliefs in the light of the outcome of actual events. Common sense beliefs are thus self-correcting. There is no absolute security for them, since there is no logical guarantee that the natural sequences to which men have become accustomed will invariably recur. But if men are to learn and profit from experience, they must take for granted that the future will resemble the past, *"that like objects, placed in like circumstances, will always produce like effects"* (T. 105). And in fact men do believe quite naturally in the uniformity of nature, although no one has ever found a rational proof of this indispensible law. But the proof is not needed for practical purposes, because men are creatures of instinct and habit, and they do not wait upon reasons to justify the inferences which they are determined by custom (i.e. conditioning) to draw. If there is any justification for allowing custom to be "the great guide of human life," (E 44), it is the purely pragmatic one that human survival depends upon it.

The common sense beliefs involved in everyday activity occur as an integral part of the responses that we have been conditioned to make upon the presentation of various sorts of stimuli. The sailor's idea of the storm — his belief in its imminence — is integrated with the conditioned response he makes to the threatening weather: trimming sail, heading into wind, battening down hatches. A strict behaviourist would say that the sailor's belief in the storm consists wholly in the action he takes to deal with it. Whether one takes this view, or regards the idea of the storm as a mental correlate of physical activity, or even as a mental cause of his behaviour, all would agree with the four chief points that Hume wants to make about a belief of this elementary kind. 1. It occurs spontaneously as a conditioned response. 2. The conditioning is the effect of having repeatedly experienced phenomena resembling the present one in association with the sort of event which is the present object of belief. 3. Such a belief is warranted by the utility value of appropriate action in the situation. 4. The belief will be directly confirmed or disconfirmed in the ensuing course of experience.

If beliefs are the natural effects of associative processes initiated by sense experiences, a conformity of belief and reality might be expected as inevitable. But it is not inevitable, nor even so usual as one less sceptical than Hume might suppose. The epistemologist is expected to provide criteria for distinguishing between tenable beliefs and groundless ones. Hume's criteria are derived from his genetic analysis of natural belief. How the defining features of common sense belief serve to identify baseless fictions can be shown by returning to the case of the sailor.

Let us ascribe to our sailor a belief in Neptune, and let us suppose that he attributes the impending storm to the god's anger. Such a belief, which Hume would call superstitious, exhibits none of the defining features of a natural belief. The sailor would not have learned about the existence of Neptune from his own observations. He would never have been directly acquainted with the god, and would not, therefore, be in a position to establish an association between Neptune's moods and storms at sea. His belief is idle; it will exert no influence on his behaviour as he prepares to negotiate a rough sea. No future experience will tend either to confirm or disconfirm his belief, for it is equally compatible with any condition of weather that might ensue. In short, a superstitious belief, unlike a natural one, is not grounded in experience, not useful, and not verifiable.

The antithesis of superstition for Hume is science. In his view, which was the view also of Bacon and of Hobbes, methods of natural science have evolved from common sense procedures which have come into use for solving practical problems that arise in the everyday lives of men who live close to nature. The methodology of science, when made explicit, simply formalizes the principles which govern the thinking of men who have learned to profit from experience. Experience provides indifferently grist for the mill of fancy and of understanding, and the imagination is responsible both for fictions and for those authentic ideas, faithful copies of previous sense impressions, through which we become aware of absent things. If we are to acquire trustworthy beliefs, we need rules to discipline the imagination. These rules are simply generalizations about the conditions that obtain when reliable inferences are made. A man learns that heat causes water to boil by observing that boiling consistently follows the application of heat. From a variety of similar experiences, through which he learns how to predict and control various phenomena, he also learns such general rules as that the same cause invariably produces the same effect, unless some other factor intervenes. When these rules which tacitly govern thinking in everyday life are combined with selective observation and experimental control, the transition is made from common sense to science.

If men restricted their beliefs about the world to what they have learned from their own experience, or from the experimentally verified discoveries of the scientists, they would not go far astray. For even when they make hasty generalizations, overlook factors that will impede the normal progress of a familiar causal sequence, or base conclusions upon hopes or fears rather than upon evidence, so long as their thinking bears upon the empirical realities bound up with their practical lives, their errors will soon enough be brought home to them. Risk of incorrigible error increases progressively the further thinking becomes removed from practical designs in the immediate environment. Men could not have derived their more improbable, persistent beliefs from first hand experience. What, then, is the principal source of erroneous belief? Hume answers in one word: "Education."

> I am persuaded, that upon examination we shall find more
> than one half of those opinions, that prevail among
> mankind, to be owing to education, and that the principles,
> which are thus implicitly embrac'd, aver-ballance those,

which are owing either to abstract reasoning or experience. As liars, by the frequent repetition of their lies, come at last to remember [believe?] them; so the judgement, or rather the imagination, by the like means, may have ideas so strongly imprinted on it, and conceive them in so full a light, that they may operate upon the mind in the same manner with those, which the senses, memory or reason present to us. But as education is an artificial and not a natural cause, and as its maxims are frequently contrary to reason, and even to themselves in different times and places, it is never upon that account recogniz'd by philosophers; tho' in reality it be built almost on the same foundation of custom and repetition as our reasonings from causes and effects. (T 117)

When Hume says that education is "built *almost* on the same foundation" as learning from experience, he is pointing both to a similarity and to a difference between these two ways of acquiring beliefs about the world. The common factor is repetition. The distinguishing factor resides in the original stimuli. Natural beliefs are based upon observing recurrent natural sequences. Artificial beliefs are based upon associations fixed by reiterated verbal presentations. Men are accustomed to thunder following lightning, and therefore expect thunder whenever they see lightning. They have been conditioned. A habit has been instilled. Men are repeatedly told that wolves are vicious hunters of human beings, and therefore expect to be attacked whenever they encounter wolves. They have been in-doctrinated. The ideas of wolf and danger have become associated. The natural belief originates in sense experience. The idea which anticipates the thunder is a copy of previous sense impressions. The artificial belief originates in statements heard or read. The idea of danger is a copy of an idea — of someone else's idea communicated by words.[4]

---

4. T 115-16: "that custom, to which I attribute all belief and reasoning, may operate upon the mind in invigorating an idea after two several ways. For supposing that in all past experience we have found two objects to have been always conjoin'd together, 'tis evident, that upon the appearance of one of these objects in an impression, we must from custom make an easy transition to the idea of that object, which usually attends it; and by means of the present impression and easy transition must conceive that idea in a stronger and more lively manner, than we do any loose floating image of the fancy. But let us next

Hume had set himself the customary philosophical task of correcting false beliefs about the world. In most instances he is not concerned with replacing false beliefs with true ones, but with showing that there are no good grounds upon which to base any belief at all. The usual upshot of a Humean argument is that the question over which learned opinions differ is unanswerable — quite beyond the powers of human understanding. The reason why permanent suspension of judgement is required in these cases is that no experiences will ever be forthcoming to confirm or deny purely speculative opinions. Many beliefs acquired from educators are of this unverifiable sort; and the clear implication of Hume's empiricist theory of knowledge is that such beliefs should be discarded.

Most prominent in the set of disposable ideas were almost all the doctrines included in courses of religious education in Hume's time. No human experience provides any basis for evaluating the truth of teachings about the origins of creation, the ultimate reasons of why things are as they are, the destiny of the soul, divine interventions in the course of nature, providential intercessions in human affairs, and the like.

Vulnerable to indoctrination though he may be, every man needs teachers, because what he can learn about the world from personal experience extends only to what he observes and remembers. It may be a picturesque truth (or half truth) that each civilized man goes through again the educative process of the race. But if he can learn in a few short years what it took his ancestors aeons to master, that is because he does not need to re-discover everything for himself. He can be taught, and man must

suppose, that a mere idea alone, without any of this curious and almost artificial preparation, shou'd frequently make its appearance in the mind, this idea must by degrees acquire a facility and force; and both by its firm hold and easy introduction distinguish itself from any new and unusual idea. This is the only particular, in which these two kinds of custom agree; and if it appear, that their effects on the judgment are similar and proportionable, we may certainly conclude, that the foregoing explication of that faculty is satisfactory. But can we doubt of this agreement in their influence on the judgment, when we consider the nature and effects of education?
All those opinions and notions of things, to which we have been accustom'd from our infancy, take such deep root, that 'tis impossible for us, by all the powers of reason and experience, to eradicate them; and this habit not only approaches in its influence, but even on many occasions prevails over that which arises from the constant and inseparable union of causes and effects."

be taught, if human knowledge is to advance at all, generation to generation. Hume does not mean that because much insupportable nonsense is taught, teachers should be banished. He means to confine their instruction in matters of fact to areas in which it is possible to determine whether what is taught is true or false.

Natural science occupies one such area, and history another. It is an integral part of a scientific education to learn that art of experimenting which enables the student to satisfy himself about what is presented as truth about the world.[5] The personal experience upon which the student of history relies is of a more general nature. What he chiefly needs for the critical assessment of historical claims is an understanding of human nature such as comes only from long experience of men and affairs.[6]

Of the many abuses of authority Hume particularly detested the imposition of belief. In *The Natural History of Religion* he has harsh and bitter things to say about the demoralizing effects of indoctrination.[7] The clear suggestion of these remarks is that

5. Hume's confidence in the layman's preparedness to pass judgement on scientific claims was not so misplaced in his own time as it would be today. It was open to any reader of *The Starry Messenger* to confirm Galileo's astronomical observations by following his instructions for making a telescope ("spyglass") given early in the book. Similarly, he could verify Galileo's theorems in mechanics by conducting the experiments described in *Dialogues Concerning Two New Sciences*. In his *Discourse on Method,* Part V, Descartes advised his readers on the dissection of the heart of a mammal. From his first scientific publication ("A New Theory of Light and Colours") to his last (*Opticks*) Newton was scrupulous in explaining the experimental procedures to be followed for verifying his conclusions.

6. History presents peculiar difficulties to the extent that its claims are based upon testimony, as Hume explains in the essay "Of Miracles" (E S.10). When judging a historical claim, the reader must rely upon his own experience for estimating both the intrinsic probability of the event and the probity of the witness. "No man can have any other experience but his own," Hume observed in a letter to Hugh Blair. 'The experience of others becomes his only by the credit which he gives to their testimony; which proceeds from his own experience of human nature" (*The Letters of David Hume*, 2 vols., ed. J.Y.T. Greig (Oxford, Clarendon Press, 1932), I, 349. (Subsequent volume and page references to *The Letters . . .*, abbreviated as "L" follow quotations in parentheses.) For an example of Hume's own scrupulous objectivity as a historian see Notes G and H to Ch. XLII of *The History of England* in which Hume considers whether the conspiratorial letters by which Mary, Queen of Scots, was convicted of high treason were genuine or forgeries.

7. Ed. Richard Wollheim, *Hume on Religion* (London and Glasgow:

the intellectually honest teacher provides evidence and arguments for the claims he makes about reality, leaving people free to judge for themselves in the light of their own experience.

II

When Hume was serving as personal secretary to Lord Hertford, Ambassador to the Court of France, he was visited by one of his oldest and closest friends, Sir Gilbert Elliot of Minto. Elliot had hoped to find a school in Paris for his two sons, but had left the city before choosing one. On his journey homeward he wrote on September 15, 1764 from Brussels asking Hume to search for the most suitable school in which to settle the boys.

Hume took his commission seriously, and immediately set about to inspect schools recommended by his many Parisian friends. In a letter dated just one week later than Elliot's, he reports the first results of his investigations. Hume's criteria of a good school appear between the lines of this letter and several others which quickly followed it. A school suitable for young gentlemen should be located in a fashionable district, near to open country for exercise, attended by persons of quality, kept clean, orderly, and disciplined, and it should be cheap. With these amenities — social, hygienic, economic — secured, there remains the question of the qualities to be sought in teachers and headmaster. The terms in which Hume commends such persons indicate his standards. Of Madame Anson's school, eventually disqualified by reason of its unfashionable location and remoteness from "all Walks and Places of Exercise" (L I 468), he reports that he "found that Family a very decent, sensible kind of People" (loc. cit.), and, in his next letter, that they seemed "a discreet, sober Set of People" (L I 472). Of another potential custodian he writes, "I have heard a very good Character of Erivot, Professor of Rhetoric in The College de Beavais . . ." (loc. cit.). On D'Alembert's recommendation he visited the

---

Collins (Fontana)), pp. 87-88: "Among idolaters, the words may be false, and belie the secret opinion: But among more exalted religionists, the opinion itself contracts a kind of falsehood, and belies the inward sentiment. The heart secretly detests such measures of cruel and implacable vengeance; but the judgment dares not but pronounce them perfect and adorable. And the additional misery of this inward struggle aggravates all other terrors, by which those unhappy victims to superstition are for ever haunted."

school of Monsieur Bastide, who impressed him as being "a genteel, well bred man" (L I 468), but somewhat high in price. He then called upon D'Alembert's mistress for advice. His report to Elliot of this interview with Madamoiselle L'Espinasse ("really one of the most sensible women in Paris" ibid. 469) suggests that excellence of moral character in a teacher counted for more with Hume than strength of intellect:

> She told me that there could not be a worthier, honester, better Man, than Bastide. I told her that I had entertained the same Opinion of him; but was afraid his Head-piece was none of the best. She own'd that he did not excel in that Side; and a proof it was, that he had wrote several Books, all of which were below middling. On my return home, I found the enclosed letter from him. I have promised him an Answer by the Return of the Post from England. (loc. cit.)

In the end the Elliot boys were settled in La Pension Militaire. Hume's recommendation of this school reads in part as follows:

> I found there an excellent airy House, with an open Garden belonging to it. It is the last House but one in Paris; has a Prospect & Access into the large open space of the Invalides, & from thence into the Fields. The Number of boys is limited to thirty five, whom I saw in the Court, in a blue Uniform with a narrow silver Lace: They left off their Play and made me a Bow with the best Grace in the world, as I pass'd. I was carry'd to their Master, the Abbé Choquart, who appeared to me a sensible, judicious, sedate Man, agreeable to the Character I had receivd of him. He carry'd me through the Boys' Apartments, which were cleanly, light, spacious, & each lay in a small Bed apart. I saw a large Collection of Instruments for experimental Philosophy. I saw an ingenious Machine for teaching Chronology. There were Plans of Fortification. While I was considering these, I heard a Drum beat in the Court: It was the hour for assembling the Boys for their military Exercises. I went down. They had now all got on their Belts, and had their Muskets in their hands. They went thro' all the Prussian Exercise with the best Air & greatest Regularity imaginable. Almost all were about your Sons' Age; a Year or two more or less. They are the Youth of the best Quality

in France: A Newphew of M. de Choiseul: two Newphews of M. de Beringhen. In short of the first Families. Their Air & Manner seem to bespeak it. (L I 472-73)

Near the end of what has survived of this autograph, Hume mentions another merit of La Pension Militaire:

Your sons need never go to Mass unless they please, and nobody shall ever talk to them about Religion.

After a few months Elliot has become anxious about the moral hazards of residency in France, and on March 25, 1765 he writes to ask if Hume thinks that continuing there "will not be of prejudice to them, and render them too much french men" (L I 499 n. 2). He expresses concern also about Robert Liston, tutor to the boys: "I own," he writes, "I am more apprehensive of the consequences of a Paris life upon a young man of his age than upon the boys, who are too young to enter into the full dissipation of a country where not to be dissipated is hardly to have an existence . . ." Hume replies that he finds "Mr. Liston's conduct not only irreproachable, but laudable" and that "the Abbé praises him (and with great reason, as appears to me) for his Reserve, his Modesty, His good Sense, his Sobriety, and his Virtue" (ibid. 500).

About three weeks later Hume writes again to report his attendance at the Examination of l'Abbé Choquart's School — at a Visitors' Day, in other words. After complimenting the elder son's flawless accent, displayed while demonstrating theorems of geometry, Hume adds:

There was also one Circumstance of your young Gentlemen's Behaviour with which I was much pleasd; but whether you will take the Praise of it to yourself, or ascribe it partly to the Imitation of French Manners, I cannot determine. I arrived a little before the Commencement of the Examination; and, walking into the Garden, I took Shelter, from the Heat, under some Trees. Your young Gentlemen, as soon as they saw men, ran & brought me a Chair, which they plac'd carefully in the most shady Spot they could find. I doubt this Attention woud not be very common among mere English Schoolboys. (ibid. 502)

The impression left by these letters is that Hume conceived of education as preparation for life in society. Healthful exercise and sound training in manners and morals made the core of any curriculum of which he would approve. His enthusiasm for Prussian drill, somewhat surprising in a philosopher, was balanced by the stress he put upon the proficient teaching of languages. The Elliot boys' mastery of French counted heavily in his endorsement of La Pension Militaire.

Hume was repratriated to the British Isles in January of 1766. In the summer of the following year, he is investigating Norlands School on behalf of another anxious father, Baron Mure of Caldwell. Hume questions the headmaster, Graffigni, on his method of teaching Latin. Persuaded that the method is "whimsical," he tests it by returning to the school to interview the two pupils:

> I endeavoured to inform myself concerning their Progress in Latin. I find that they are not taught any Latin Grammar. They are only instructed in the Sense of single detached Words, which they learn both in Greek and Latin at once: Accordingly they told me Water, aqua, νδωρ but tho' I tryd them in about half a dozen more words, I coud not find their Learning extended so far. All this appears to me very whimsical; and I doubt a dead Language can never be learnt in this manner without Grammar. In a living Language the continual Application of the Words and Phrazes teaches at the same time the Sense of the Words and their Reference to each other; but a List of Words got by heart, without any connected Sense, easily escapes the Memory, and is but a small Part of the Language. (L II 157)

Given the Baron's conviction about the consummate importance of Latin, Hume might have been expected to recommend withdrawal. But he advises according to his own priorities:

> But tho' I suspect this Man in general to be empty and conceited, as your boys are so very young, their time is not very precious; and provided that they be well in point of Health and Morals or rather manners (which seem to me unexceptionable) you may allow them to remain there some time without Anxiety. (loc. cit.)

In a letter to Baron Mure the following year, when Graffigni had been banished and replaced by his Latin master, Elin, Hume observes, ironically, but making a serious point, "the Loss of

Graffigni may be felt. By his profound Study of the Human Mind he had discovered that Decency and good Manners are very proper to be inculcated in boys, and was more attentive to that point than perhaps Elin will be, who, with a sounder Understanding, has had a more vulgar Education" (L II 188).

III

We saw earlier that as an epistemologist Hume advocated the autonomy of the individual intellect. In common sense matters the individual is right to rely upon his own experience. With respect to the matters of fact treated in natural science and history, he ought to decide for himself on the basis of evidence what to believe. From the teachings of metaphysicians and theologians he ought to withhold assent: for he will find in his own experience no means of determining whether what is taught is correct or mistaken. The purpose of study, so far as matters of fact are concerned, is to acquire beliefs which conform to what is actually the case in the world and to what really happened in the past. Since Hume thought that some of the most influential doctrines concerning nature and concerning the past were untenable, we may suppose that he would have approved of an education which cultivated a critical, sceptical, self-reliant mind. These were the conspicuous merits of his own intellect which students of his work usually acquire to some degree.

The purpose of education on the intellectual side is to learn to make correct judgements. The purpose of moral training is to learn correct behaviour. But the sense which "correct" bears in an intellectual context differs profoundly from the meaning that the term acquires in the context of manners and morals. When we speak of correct statements or judgements, reports or results, accounts or descriptions, we mean that what is said, the proposition expressed, conforms to what is in fact the case. When we speak of correct behaviour, of correct manners or morals, deportment or conduct, or even of correct usage or pronunciation, we mean that what is done or said conforms to accepted social conventions.

According to Hume's ethical theory, moral judgements are neither true nor false, They cannot be demonstrated, as are the analytical judgements of pure mathematics; nor can they be verified, as are the synthetic judgements of empirical science; nor can they be confirmed, as the factual claims of history may be.

Moral judgements serve to express one's feelings of liking or disliking aroused by qualities of human character manifested in behaviour. Morality is ultimately an affair of the feelings, not of the intellect. "Reason is, and ought only to be the slave of the passions . . ." (T 415), says Hume in his most notorious remark on morality. Given this irrationalist basis of his ethics, Hume might have been expected to be sceptical of the validity of moral rules, and accordingly to favour permissiveness in moral education. But as one of his biographers, Greig, has rightly emphasized, Hume's scepticism did not extend to his ethics; "as for ethics," Greig says, "David Hume accepted them [common-sense beliefs] without question," although, he continues, "Reason could not demonstrate a single one."[8] And from his letters we have learned that Hume considered the moral and social development of the pupil to be a primary responsibility of the school, and that he was willing to forgive intellectual weaknesses in teachers who were earnest about the inculcation of virtue.

In order to celebrate experience as the infallible teacher, and to account for erroneous beliefs by holding human teachers responsible for them, Hume distinguished in his epistemology between experience as a natural cause of belief and education as an artificial one. An analogous distinction between natural virtues and artificial virtues structures his ethical theory. Such natural virtues as kindness, charity, generosity, and clemency emanate from the instinctual sympathy which each human being feels for others with whom he is intimately related and upon whose approval his own happiness depends. The natural virtues are sufficient to sustain harmonious relations between an individual and his family and his friends. But human sympathy, the psychological basis of morality, is limited, and does not extend to the many members of society who are strangers. Society requires for its peace and preservation such artificial virtues as justice, patriotism, modesty, chastity, and good manners.

These artificial virtues obviously do not appear spontaneously as the individual matures, nor can they be instilled by argument. The moral educator must work upon the feelings of his charge, not upon his intellect. It is a matter of influencing attitudes, not of implanting beliefs. "Nothing," Hume writes, "can oppose or retard the impulse of passion but a contrary

8. J.Y.T. Greig, *David Hume* (London, Jonathan Cape, 1931), p. 14.

impulse . . ." (T 415). To elaborate, civilization requires each member of society to act from time to time contrary to natural impulse, and no amount of reasoning with him will ensure that he will do it if he does not feel like it. When private inclination is at odds with public good, the socially approved response can be expected only from an individual who has been thoroughly conditioned in socially desirable patterns of behavior.

> As publick praise and blame encrease our esteem for justice; so private education and instruction contribute to the same effect. For as parents easily observe, that a man is the more useful, both to himself and others, the greater degree of probity and honour he is endow'd with; and that those principles have greater force, when custom and education assist interest and reflexion: For these reasons they are induc'd to inculcate on their children, for their earliest infancy, the principles of probity, and teach them to regard the observance of those rules, by which society is maintain'd, as worthy and honourable, and their violation as base and infamous. By this means the sentiments of honour may take root in their tender minds, and acquire such firmness and solidity, that they may fall little short of those principles, which are the most essential to our natures, and the most deeply radicated in our internal constitution. (T 500-1)

To return to my starting point and to conclude: Hume's epistemology implies a progressive theory of education in subjects of purely intellectual concern. Pupils should be encouraged to test what they are taught about reality against their own experience. Indoctrination is bad. Hume's ethics enjoin a conservative theory of education. Pupils should be trained to behave according to the conventions of the society for which they are being prepared. Indoctrination is good.

Indoctrination is bad. Indoctrination is good. Only a philosopher who understood the profound difference between cultivating intellect and molding character could affirm both of these propositions without contradiction.

James Noxon

The Idea of the Inculcation
of National Patriotism
in French Educational Thought
1750-1789[1]

A nation might be defined as a group of people sharing a sense of community based on such factors as language, culture, and attachment to a particular territory. In the past such a sense of community was often overridden by adherence to various political entities smaller or larger than the nation. Men's loyalty on the one hand was focused on local units such as a town or tiny principality, or on large units such as a polyglot empire or universal church. Nationalism emerged when men's devotion became concentrated on an intermediate unit, the nation state. At times their devotion has become centred on a nation state already pieced together by a succession of rulers. At other times they have sought to bring together separate but adjacent people with a common culture to create a nation state. At still other times they have sought to break up a large multinational state in order to achieve an independent nation state. Thus men have demonstrated their nationalism by their devotion to, or desire to create, a political entity which coincided with, or would coincide with, their nation. Often too men have revealed their growing nationalism by their pride in the institutions, language, literature, art, and other accomplishments of their nation. For some, nationalism has become a veritable religion. On occasion nationalism has become so exaggerated that it has led to claims of superiority of one nation over supposedly inferior neighbours.

In France modern nationalism may not have appeared full-blown until the Revolution, but national consciousness grew steadily from the later middle ages through the early modern period until in the mid-eighteenth century something very close to nationalism emerged, what I have chosen to call 'national

1. This paper was originally written for presentation at a seminar in the History of Ideas Unit, directed by Eugene Kamenka, in the Research School of the Social Sciences, the Institute of Advanced Studies, the Australian National University, where the author was a Visiting Fellow 1974-1975. It has been considerably revised in view of discussion there and later at McMaster.

patriotism.' During the fifteenth, sixteenth, and seventeenth centuries national consciousness was mainly focused on the succession of kings who gradually pieced together much of modern France.[2] This form of patriotism, centred on the king as the embodiment of France, reached its peak under Louis XIV. The Sun King presided over the largest, wealthiest, most populated, best armed state in western Europe. And French literature, art, and architecture began to attain ascendancy throughout the continent. Patriotism focused on the monarchy was expressed in Père Gabriel Daniel's monumental *Histoire de France* in 1713. In his preface Daniel emphasized the need to base history on factual evidence, but his bias was clear. "L'histoire d'un Royaume ou d'une Nation a pour objet le Prince et l'Etat; c'est-là comme le centre où tout doit tendre et se rapporter . . . "[3] But tyrannical rule and burdensome wars during the great king's reign, followed by the regency, then the lack-lustre rule of his great-grandson, reduced the appeal of the monarchy as the focus of patriotism. As the monarchy diminished, patriotism tended to shift to what the kings had created — *la patrie* or the nation itself.

Both centrifugal and centripetal forces competed in the state which the Capetians, Valois, and Bourbons had pieced together. Underneath the superstructure of the centralized monarchy with its agents throughout the country, lay a bewildering variety of regional differences. The newer intendancies did not always coincide with the old provinces, some provinces had ancient representative estates while most had none, taxation varied greatly from region to region, customs barriers had been abolished in less than half the country, jurisdiction of the highest courts was divided into fifteen areas, customary law prevailed in the north while Roman tradition persisted in the south, and ecclesiastical divisions different from those of the state added yet further diversity. And at the bottom of the social structure, the peasants remained attached to their local communities, sustaining distinctive regional societies,

2. W. F. Church, 'France' in *National Consciousness, History, and Political Culture in Early Modern Europe*, ed. Drest Ranum, Baltimore and London, 1975.

3. Gabriel Daniel, *Histoire de France*, first ed. 1713, Nouvelle éd., 17 vols., Paris, 1755-1757, vol. I, p. xcvi.

stubbornly maintaining their particular cultures far into the nineteenth century.[4]

Nevertheless there were forces leading certain groups to aspire to greater unity within the nation state. Time itself was increasing national consciousness by building up shared experience. Much of the state had shared common rule since the later middle ages. The conquests of Louis XIV in the north and in Alsace were three-quarters of a century old. Even Lorraine, which was finally annexed in 1766, had long been under French influence and even French administration. Only Corsica was unassimilated. Moreover royal highways, radiating out from Paris, were tying this territory together and providing arteries for the diffusion of ideas. Tourist guides such as Louis Denis' *Le Conducteur français*, which featured coloured maps of these arteries, not only illustrate how they helped to unify the country, but demonstrate that some Frenchmen were becoming conscious of their importance.[5] At the same time the creation of new royal officials and increased taxation meant that the central government was impinging more directly on the lives of the people. More bureaucrats and taxes may not have aroused enthusiasm, but they did intensify awareness of the nation state.

The long series of wars between France and England stretching from the reign of Louis XIV into the French Revolution, "the second Hundred Years War" as Buffington called it, helped to increase national patriotism by stimulating a we-they feeling.[6] Embryonic nationalism had emerged during the First Hundred Years War, but at that time a unified nation state, to serve as the focus of devotion, was only in the early stages of development. Recurrent wars with England were followed by the growth of Anglophobia, partly a product of national feeling, partly a cause of its intensification. At the same time French accomplishments in literature, philosophy, art, architecture,

4. Eugen Weber, *Peasants into Frenchmen. The Modernization of Rural France 1870-1914*, Stanford, 1976.

5. Louis Denis, *Le Conducteur français*, 9 vols., Paris, 1776-1780. A shorter earlier edition entitled *Guide royal* —, 2 vols., Paris, 1774, featured a map at the end of the second volume showing the whole highway network radiating out from Paris.

6. Consciousness of the long rivalry between France and England was revealed clearly in books such as G.-H. Gaillard, *Histoire de la rivalité de la France et de l'Angleterre*, 11 vols., Paris, 1771-1777.

and various crafts, encouraged national pride. It was an age when German princes imitated Versailles, when Prussian academicians discussed why French was a superior language, when Polish magnates build *châteaux*, when many Russian noblemen preferred to speak French, and when literate classes all over the continent read French books and journals. Grimm's literary newsletter was a sign of this cultural leadership. In some Frenchmen this cultural hegemony led to a feeling of superiority, even a sense of mission.

Signs of growing nationalism appeared on all sides in the fifties and sixties. One important sign was the increased use of such words as *nation, national, patrie, patriote, patriotisme,* and *citoyen.* Only *nationalisme* did not appear until 1798. From the way writers employed the words motherland and nation, which they commonly used interchangeably, it is clear that they meant the territory encompassed by the French state.[7] Patriotism meant devotion to the nation state. And a citizen, as distinct from a subject, was someone emotionally committed to that state. Proliferation of poems with titles such as "Hommage à la Patrie" reveal that such emotional attachment to the motherland was increasing. Several patriotic plays were staged, including the consciously nationalistic drama by Belloy, *Le Siège de Calais,* significantly drawing its theme from the First Hundred Years War. Meanwhile various histories were published recounting the deeds of great Frenchmen, and even outstanding French women, with titles such as the *Plutarque français.*

At the same time in the world of art growing nationalism

7. For example in C.-A. Comte de Thélis, *Plan d'éducation nationale, en faveur des pauvres enfans de la campagne* —, s.l., 1779, pp. 16-17, note the conjunction of patriotic, national, kingdom and state: "On comprend que ce n'est qu'en formant au milieu de nous une génération toute nouvelle, et en poussant toutes les volontés vers le même but par l'accord soutenu des mêmes principes, par une éducation commune, applicable dans ses modifications aux différentes classes de citoyens, par des enseignements clairs et précis, par des leçons, par des institutions vraiment patriotiques et nationales qui se répondent d'une extrémité du royaume à l'autre, qu'on pourra venir à bout de rendre à l'Etat son ancienne énergie." In his *Règlement concernant les écoles nationales, du 12 février 1780,* Paris, s.d., p. 5 Thélis speaks of soldiers "précieux à la Patrie" trained for work "utile à l'Etat," thus associating motherland and state. Still later in Thélis' collection, *Mémoires concernant les écoles nationales,* Paris, 1781 (-1789) III, p. 31, the Chevalier de Bruni described an educational system established by the government as "donné sous les yeux de la Nation," thus linking government and nation.

revealed itself in various ways. The painter Cochin boasted about the superiority of French taste in all the arts.[8] "Ce n'est pas assez de vaincre un Peuple par les armes, nous devons triompher de tous par les talens," asserted the playwright and art critic Carmontelle; "et soit en paix, soit en guerre, ma Nation, dans aucun genre, ne doit souffir de rivalité. François que nous sommes! ce titre nous impose la loi de ne céder à personne."[9] Other art critics called on artists to choose national subjects.[10] There was in fact a gradual increase in such themes in the biennial Salons up to the Revolution. The art minister, d'Angiviller, sought to accelerate this trend by commissioning paintings of historic French events and statues of French heroes. The same minister attempted to have the royal collection turned into a national collection housed in the Louvre to create a sort of shrine. He called it his "projet national."[11]

Some architects proposed housing statues of national heroes in temples which anticipated the transformation of the church of Sainte Geneviève into the Panthéon during the revolution. On the eve of that revolution Boullée designed such a temple, inscribed with the name MUSAEUM GALLICANUM with "les statues en marbre des hommes célèbres de la Nation et celle du Roi Louis XVI régnant fixée au centre du monument."[12] Other artists produced series of images of national heroes which were sold separately or in bound volumes. One striking example was the series of engravings, mostly by Sergent-Marceau, published by Blin after 1787, entitled *Portraits des grands hommes, femmes illustres et sujets mémorables de France, gravés et imprimés en couleur*. In the three volumes eventually produced only two foreigners — Franklin and Washington — appeared among nearly two hundred French heroes such as Charlemagne, Louis IX, Charles V, St. Joan, Francis I, Henry IV, Bayard, Du

8. C.-N. Cochin, *Discours prononcé à la séance publique de l'Académie des sciences, belles-lettres et arts de Rouen en 1777*, Paris, 1777, vol. I, pp. 5-6.

9. [L.-C. Carmontelle] *Coup de patte sur le Salon de 1779, dialogue précédé et suivi de réflexions sur la peinture*, Paris, 1779, pp. 34-37.

10. Anon., *La Muette qui parle au Salon de 1781*, Bibliothèque nationale, Collection Deloynes, vol. XII, item 257, p. 6.

11. James A. Leith, "Nationalism and the Fine Arts in France 1750-1789," *Studies on Voltaire and the Eighteenth Century*, vol. LXXXIX, 1972, pp. 919-37.

12. "Musée français projetté, "Bibliothèque Nationale. Cabinet des Estampes. Ha 56 No. 47.

Guesclin, Coligny, Sully, Catinat, Vauban, and Jean Bart.[13]

Even the advocates of urban renewal revealed the growth of national patriotism. In the late sixties Maille Dussausoy published two large tomes calling for a whole series of public works in the capital which would then serve as a model for provincial centres. He held up the example of the Athenians and Romans who sought to glorify their motherlands through great monuments. His plan included market places, hospitals, theatres, and parks. One of his major proposals was that the Louvre be completed to house the city hall, the academies, the royal library, and the biennial art exhibits. The surrounding squares would be designed to accommodate public festivals. The completed Louvre and new squares would become the centre of an impressive chain of more than thirty palaces and public buildings. Dussausoy repeatedly emphasized how such an impressive centre for the capital would glorify France. It was not so much the monarchy as the nation which this planner sought to extol — he appeals to *Ma Nation* to demonstrate French taste. If his plan were adopted, Paris would overawe visitors and the Louvre would become the immortal shrine of the Nation (always capitalized).[14]

In the political sphere nationalism was also increasingly apparent. In eighteenth-century France the highest courts were the dozen *parlements* plus three sovereign councils. Created by the kings as they built up a monarchical state, each court had jurisdiction over a certain region, the largest being the *parlement* of Paris, controlling about a third of France. Although originally creatures of the king, these sovereign courts claimed to protect France from arbitrary government, using as their principal weapon their power to register all laws. Despite the fact that they had different jurisdictions, these courts gradually developed a sense of solidarity, sometimes claimed to constitute a single body, and professed to represent *la nation*. It was these courts which led the assault on the Jesuit Order in the early sixties. The Order was attacked for its moral teachings, its political ideas, and its tyrannical rules, but above all for constituting a great subversive

13. Pierre Blin, *Portraits des grands hommes, femmes illustres, et sujets mémorables de France, gravés et imprimés en couleur,* Paris, [1787-1792].

14. Maille Dussausoy, *Le Citoyen désintéressé, ou diverses idées patriotiques concernant quelques établissements et embellissements utiles à la ville de Paris,* Paris, 1767-1768.

international organization teaching loyalty to a foreign ruler. Contemporary caricatures depicted the Order as a giant tree spreading its branches around states throughout the world. The Order was thus suppressed partly because it was seen as a threat to the nation state.

One striking example of the intensification of national sentiment in the political sphere was an essay by Mathon de la Cour, a member of the Academy of Lyon and other learned societies, entitled *Discours sur les meilleurs moyens de faire naître et d'encourager le patriotisme dans une monarchie*, which won the essay contest on this subject sponsored by the Academy of Châlons-sur-Marne in 1787. By patriotism the author meant what we would call nationalism because he constantly speaks of devotion to the nation. He complained that exaggerated emphasis on the patriotism of classical republics had encouraged the antinational notion that patriotism could not flourish in a monarchical state such as France. On the contrary he contended that patriotism could thrive under a monarchy if the king would work for the welfare of all the people, strive to improve the moral tone of the nation, curb excessive inequalities, and above all give his subjects an active role in helping to administer the country. The king would then become the centre of patriotic devotion. Mathon also proposed arousing patriotism by distributing various rewards for public service at local festivals — *fêtes nationales* he sometimes calls them — at which the king himself would sometimes appear. The emotions aroused would have a permanent impact, especially on young people. "Au milieu de cette ivresse générale, les jeunes surtout, émus et enchantés feroient cent fois le serment de n'exister que pour la patrie, et tout sacrifier au désir de mériter de tels honneurs."[15]

But perhaps the most striking sign of rising nationalism was the hope of inculcating national sentiment through public education. And as this aspiration emerged, educational reformers for the first time realized the full potentiality of print as a means of moulding a like-minded citizenry. In recent years Marshall McLuhan and his disciples have called attention to the impact of print on western civilization. On the one hand they

15. C.-J. Mathon de la Cour, *Discours sur les meilleurs moyens de faire naître et d'encourager le patriotisme dans une monarchie* —, Paris, 1788, p. 47.

have argued that print has promoted individualism because one usually reads a book alone, whereas oral communication involves group participation. However they have also pointed out that print made possible the organization of society in a new way. By providing a uniform repeatable means of delivering messages, movable type provided a uniform repeatable method of training citizens. Print not only made possible the teaching of reading in a uniform way, but also the standardization of what the reader read. Print thus made available a tremendous potential power for the creation of sameness in society. "What we might call homogeneity of citizenship," asserts one McLuhanite. "By similar training and uniform educational patterns you could create a kind of manpower pool of almost replaceable parts."[16]

However even in the fifties and sixties some outstanding educational thinkers had not realized the means which might be used to engender a national outlook throughout France. In fact the most celebrated book on education in the sixties, Rousseau's *Emile, ou de l'éducation*, 1762, which provoked widespread controversy and went through more than twenty editions in ten years, proposed a system of domestic education aimed at preserving as much as possible of the natural propensities of the child. At the beginning of the book Rousseau claimed that since there was no motherland, consequently no citizens, there could be no genuine public education.[17] But when he was advocating moulding a citizen, rather than preserving a natural man, he strongly advocated public education as a means of engendering support for the general will and attachment to *la patrie*. Thus in the article "Economie politique," which appeared in Diderot's *Encyclopédie* back in 1755, Rousseau had asserted that public education was certainly "la plus importante affaire de l'Etat."[18] But he had not proposed any specific state machinery or standardized textbooks to produce patriotic citizens.

Even La Chalotais, whose *Essai d'éducation nationale*,

16. Robert Shafer in a discussion with Marshall McLuhan reprinted in *McLuhan Hot and Cool*, ed. by G. E. Stearn, N.Y. 1967, p. 144. See also Chapter 18, "The Printed Word: Architect of Nationalism," in M. McLuhan, *Understanding Media: the Extensions of Man*, New York, 1964.

17. J.-J. Rousseau, *Emile, ou de l'éducation* in his *Oeuvres Complètes*, Edition de la Pléiade, Paris, 1959-69, Vol. IV, pp. 250-51.

18. J.-J. Rousseau, "Sur l'économie politique" in *Oeuvres Complètes*, Edition de la Pléiade, Paris, 1959-69, Vol. III, pp. 260-61.

1763, was the first to use the adjective "national" to describe his educational system, did not propose adequate means to achieve his goal. As one of the principal leaders in the campaign to suppress the Jesuit Order in France, the Breton magistrate condemned an educational system dominated by religious orders which consequently encouraged attachment to a foreign power rather than devotion to the national state. "Ainsi l'enseignement de la Nation entière, cette portion de la législation qui est la base et le fondement des Etats," he complained, "étoit resté sous la direction immédiate d'un Régime, nécessairement ennemi de nos Lois."[19] But despite his advocacy of civic education which would encourage love for *la patrie*, La Chalotais, like Rousseau, did not propose a national system of schools. In fact at one point he remarked that domestic education might even be better than public education if good textbooks were available.[20] And although he called for composition of new textbooks on various subjects, he did not suggest any way by which the state could oversee their production.[21]

Others however were proposing some sort of government agency to create a uniform educational system throughout France. For example, in 1765 in a series of articles entitled "De l'éducation nationale" in the physiocratic journal, the *Ephémérides du citoyen*, the Abbé Baudeau called for creation of a central bureau to examine all the proposals which were pouring out in order to frame a law for French schools.[22] His terminology was especially significant. "La Nation attend un système universel, uniforme et invariable de législation pour toute espèce d'Ecoles publiques, un Code entier des Etudes; c'est le voeu de tous les bons Patriotes."[23] Baudeau called for five

19. L. R. Caradeuc de la Chalotais, *Essai d'éducation nationale, ou plan d'études pour la jeunesse*, s.l. 1763, p. 13.

20. *Ibid.*, pp. 33-34. J.-B.-L. Crevier, *Difficultés proposées à M. Le Caradeuc de la Chalotais — sur le mémoire intitulé "Essai d'éducation nationale" —*, Paris, 1763, criticized La Chalotais for exaggerating what could be accomplished at home with good textbooks and cited Saint-Pierre on the need for trained teachers in a *public* system of education.

21. Op. cit., pp. 31-32.

22. L'Abbé Nicolas Baudeau, 'De l'éducation nationale,' *Ephémérides du citoyen*, vol. I, no. 7, 25 nov. 1765, pp. 97-112; vol. II, no. 5, 17 janvier 1766, pp. 65-80; vol. III, no. 2, 7 mars 1766, pp. 17-32; vol. IV, no. 4, 12 mai 1766, pp. 49-64; vol. V, nos. 10-13, 4 août — 15 août 1766, pp. 145-208.

23. *Ibid.*, vol. I, no. 7, pp. 100-01.

different sorts of public schools for the different classes — the royal family, the nobility, the upper bourgeoisie, the lesser bourgeoisie, and the lower classes — but he emphasized the necessity to instill patriotism in the upper classes because they would provide models for the masses. The people were naturally imitators.[24]

Three years later, in a report to the Paris *parlement*, Rolland d'Erceville proposed practical means for achieving national education. During the following decade and a half Rolland produced a number of other reports which were eventually published as a collection which he called his *Plan d'éducation*. The Paris magistrate envisaged a vast educational network in which the University of Paris, in conjunction with the *parlement*, would guide the provincial universities, these universities along with the regional *parlements* would supervise the colleges in their areas, and the colleges in turn would oversee lesser educational institutions. Although the Paris *parlement* has often been depicted as the champion of provincial rights, Rolland wanted by exposing all Frenchmen to the same basic indoctrination eventually to obliterate the regional differences which separated them. He described the creation of such a common national outlook as *cette révolution*.[25] Moreover to achieve this uniformity and to ensure that patriotic and monarchical principals were taught, he stressed the need for new textbooks produced under government supervision. He called for appointment to the royal council of a new official who would oversee the whole educational system. This official would direct the production of textbooks, in fact at first this would be almost his sole task.[26]

There were at least 120 proposals for educational reform in the three decades prior to the Revolution. The reformers differed on many issues — the place of Latin in the curriculum, the role of religion, the desirability or not of having secular teachers, and so on — but the great majority demanded some sort of state

24. Ibid., p. 112.
25. B. G. Rolland d'Erceville, *Recueil de plusieurs ouvrages de M. le Président Rolland, imprimé en exécution des délibérations du Bureau d'administration du Collège Louis-le-Grand des 17 janvier et 18 avril 1782*, Paris, 1783. The reports begin in 1768. pp. 22-24.
26. On textbooks Ibid., pp. 128-29, 140-43, 184-85, 216-23 and 770-71.

system which would inculcate a national outlook. A typical exponent of this objective was the abbé Coyer, author of a *Plan d'éducation publique*, 1770. The abbé explicitly rejected Rousseau's preference for private education designed to preserve the man of Nature. No doubt it was necessary to deviate as little as possible from Nature. "Mais enfin il est nécessaire de la plier au bien général de la société," he contended, "et de ne pas blesser celle-ci, en soutenant les droits de celle-là."[27] He wanted his state program aimed at shaping children for the motherland and to begin when the child was four. And like so many others in this period, to create a homogeneous citizenry, he called for uniformity throughout France in curriculum, textbooks, methodology, language, and even dress. Above all Coyer wanted new textbooks commissioned by the government.[28]

Coyer also advocated organization of the classroom in a way which would facilitate standardization of citizens. Like most other educational reformers under the Old Regime he still defended an hierarchical social order. In fact he had a profound fear of creating too much social mobility by over-educating manual workers. With too much learning men would abandon those menial tasks essential to society. "Et la terre, qui est-ce qui la cultivera? Celui qui n'aura rien appris," Coyer replied. "L'ignorance, qui serait un mal dans les villes, est un bien au village." Consequently he advocated an hierarchical structure of schools mirroring the existing social structure. But inside the schools he wanted all children stripped of any sign of their class origins or their parents' profession so that they would in a sense revert to the state of nature. In fact Coyer even speaks of notre *République d'enfans*.[29] In hoping to strip schoolchildren of all social distinctions, he intended to make them equally susceptible to moulding by the nation state.

Among the scores of would-be educational reformers Turgot deserves special mention because of the importance of his ministry early in the reign of Louis XVI. The finance minister's proposals appear in a memorandum on municipalities, probably presented to the king in 1775. Actually the reforms which he proposed went much further than the title of the memorandum

27. (L'Abbé G.-F. Coyer) *Plan d'éducation publique*, Paris, 1770, pp. ix-x.
28. Ibid., pp. 269-75.
29. Ibid., pp. 227-235 and 276-81.

suggests. He called for a whole hierarchy of representative assemblies — parish, municipal, district, provincial, and national — which would apportion taxes and make administrative decisions. He claimed that this system would create the sense of unity presently lacking in France, but to lay the psychological basis for the system he advocated a national network of schools under a new government department. This National Council would supervise all educational institutions — academies, universities, colleges, and primary schools or *petites écoles*. This network of schools would be designed to turn out zealous citizens. For this purpose uniform textbooks prescribed by the government would be essential. "Il ferait composer dans cet esprit les livres classiques d'après un plan suivi, de manière que l'un conduisît à l'autre," Turgot wrote, "et que l'étude des devoirs du Citoyen, membre d'une famille et de l'Etat, fût le fondement de toutes les autres études, qui seront rangées dans l'ordre de l'utilité dont elles peuvent être à la Patrie." Above all the new system, with its psychological foundation, would create a uniformity of patriotic ideals.[30]

As we have seen, French eighteenth-century educational reformers would have agreed with McLuhan and his disciples on the potential power of print, but they would have profoundly disagreed with the McLuhanites that the important thing is the impact of the medium itself, not the content which it conveys. Content does not really matter — the medium is the message. McLuhanites claim that different media alter sense ratios, mental patterns, and social behaviour. They contend that print, for example, exaggerates the importance of the eye over other senses, encourages a linear sequential type of reasoning, induces a tendency to think in terms of standardized units, engenders a feeling for temporal rather than spatial relations, and so on. In contrast, like all propagandists, French eighteenth-century educational reformers cared above all about the message which the various media conveyed, whether oral, printed, visual or musical. It was in order to manipulate content that most of them advocated state control. And they were especially anxious to increase national content.

30. A.-R.-J. Turgot, 'Mémoire au Roi sur les municipalités,' *Oeuvres de M. Turgot*, 9 vols., Paris, 1808-1811, vol. VII, pp. 386-484. On education see pp. 395-98.

Encouragement of patriotism and attachment to the state could be achieved directly by civic textbooks, or indirectly by examples drawn from literature or history. Although in his essay on the best educational system for France, an essay which won a prize in a contest sponsored by the *Académie des Jeux floraux* in 1763, the priest Navarre emphasized the need for a Christian foundation for morality, he actually said much more about political virtues than Christian ones:

> Pourquoi donc nos Enfans n'apprendroient-ils pas de leurs Maîtres, non-seulement à être Chrétiens et sociables, mais à être Citoyens? Pourquoi l'éducation littéraire ne serviroit-elle pas à multiplier, parmi nos neveux, le prodige des vertus politiques? pourquoi tant d'Etudes arides et infructueuses feroient-elles négliger l'Etude sublime des devoirs de la Patrie? Pourquoi en France comme à Lacédémone, à Athènes, dans la Chine, nos collèges ne deviendroient-ils pas des Ecoles de Patriotisme?[31]

Navarre advocated inculcating devotion to the King and France through literature and history. He called the change he advocated *une révolution littéraire.*[32]

Educational reformers commonly demanded that French — *la langue nationale* as some of them called it — be given a much more important place relative to Latin and Greek which dominated the traditional curriculum. For example in 1764 in a book advocating national education under state supervision, Guyton de Morveau, attorney general in the *parlement* of Burgundy, contended that Latin and Greek were still valuable because they provided a permanent standard of good taste and were useful in various professions, but that French deserved much more attention. Consequently he proposed teaching all the subjects where content was important — mythology, history, philosophy, and science — in French. In rhetoric too most of the examples should be in French. And in poetry, while conceding the value of Latin models, he again stressed the importance of

---

31. Le P. Jean Navarre, *Discours qui a remporté le prix par le jugement de l'Académie des jeux floraux, en l'année 1763, sur ces paroles: 'Quel seroit en France le plan d'études le plus avantageux?'* s.l., 1763, p. 24.
32. Ibid., pp. 24-27.

selections in French "pour que l'intelligence soit plus sûre et le sentiment plus vif, pour cultiver aussi l'idiome maternel, et acquérir cette érudition nationale si nécessaire à tout François."[33] Others subsequently went much further in calling for a reduction in the time spent on the classical languages to make way for French. Some conservatives claimed that this assault on Latin masked an attack on the church, but the campaign for the national language simply intensified.

Most of the reformers also wanted to manipulate the teaching of history in order to engender attachment to France. This was a marked change from the position of Charles Rollin, Rector of the University of Paris, who back in 1726 had published the classical defense of the traditional curriculum. The Rector had confessed that the history of France was neglected, but he could find no time for it in the curriculum. He had suggested that by citing some outstanding deeds from time to time the teacher might inspire students to study the history of France in their leisure time.[34] By the sixties the priorities had shifted. In 1764 a priest, Ger Sertaine, complained that at present the colleges produced graduates who were foreigners in their own countries; consequently he called for more French history.[35] A year later in a book provocatively entitled *Le Temps perdu, ou les écoles publiques*, Maubert de Gouvest, who significantly called himself a patriot, likewise advocated more French history as a means of arousing patriotism and creating an "esprit national."[36] Some educators feared history since it contained so many examples of immorality, but the majority

33. L. B. Guyton de Morveau, *Mémoire sur l'éducation publique avec le prospectus d'un collège suivant les principes de cet ouvrage*, s.l. 1764, p. 221.

34. Charles Rollin, *Traité des études*, in *Oeuvres complètes*, ed. M. Letronne, Paris, 1821-25, 30 vol., vol. XXV-XXVIII (First published in 1726) Vol. XXVII, pp. 12-13. Rollin confessed that he himself had not studied enough French history and was ashamed to be "en quelque sorte étranger dans ma propre patrie."

35. [Le Père Ger Sutaine] *Plan d'études et d'éducation avec un discours sur l'éducation*, Paris, 1764, pp. 171-72. Jean-Jacques Garnier, *De l'éducation civile*, Paris, 1765, p. 219, also described graduates as "étrangers dans leur patrie."

36. J. H. Maubert de Gouvest, *Le temps perdu, ou les écoles publiques. Considérations d'un patriote sur l'éducation de la première jeunesse en France avec l'idée et le précis de l'instruction qui y serait donnée*, Amsterdam, 1765, pp. 126-33.

thought history could be very useful to inculcate morality and patriotism, especially if the episodes studied were carefully selected.[37] To give history greater relevance some reformers advocated working backwards from recent French history.

Like the Church before them, the educational thinkers thought that outstanding men or women could provide effective behavioural models. La Chalotais already called for a French Plutarch glorifying national heroes, and as we have seen several such books actually appeared.[38] Many educators were multi-media men. They wanted such heroes celebrated, not only in prose, but in poetry, songs and imagery. Citing the examples of ancient Israel, Athens, and Rome, Coyer argued that music had a profound influence on the human mind. "Si nous avions des loix politiques, bien simples, bien claires, bien arrêtées, nos Elèves les chanteraient, s'en nourriraient," he argued. "Mais au défaut des loix, ils chanteront les vertus, la justice, la bien-faisance, le désintéressement, l'amour du travail, l'amour de la patrie, qui sont les objets des loix. Ils chanteront aussi nos hommes illustres."[39] Others proposed displaying pictures of national heroes on classroom walls. Still others proposed using local patriots to inspire emulation among the citizenry. In a book on popular education published in 1783 Philipon de la Madeleine proposed periodic collections of examples of civic devotion in each parish, collections which could be read publicly at local festivals. He called these periodicals "ces annales patriotiques."[40]

Reformers valued other subjects for their potential con-tribution to nationalism. For example the Abbé Auger em-phasized physical training, not just to produce healthy in-dividuals, but to turn out vigorous young men ready to serve *la Patrie.*[41] The Comte de Thélis and others called for military drill, combined with national indoctrination, to create citizen

37. Richard de Bury, *Essai historique et moral sur l'éducation françoise,* Paris, 1777, pp. 41-54, calls for a collection of inspirational episodes chosen from ancient and modern times, but especially from the history of France. The last section of the book — pp. 417-507 — again stresses French history.

38. La Chalotais, *op. cit.,* p. 92.

39. Coyer, *op. cit.,* pp. 222-23.

40. Louis Philipon de la Madeleine, *Vues patriotiques sur l'éducation du peuple tant des villes que de la campagne; avec beaucoup de notes intéressantes,* Lyon, 1783, pp. 284-92.

soldiers.[42] Borrelly wanted students in ethics to be taught patriotism, including the proposition that suicide was an outrage, not so much against God, but against the motherland.[43] Reformers stressed the study of the geography of France as a means of making the student intimately acquainted with his homeland. Educators sometimes advocated special courses on Gallican Liberties, that is the traditional rights of the national church, in order to counter the ultramontanism recently taught by the Jesuits and still propagated by other religious orders. Others suggested that even art classes could be used to arouse national sentiments by assigning students to depict French heroes or military victories. And some lamented the fact that outside of school there were no temples, altars, or sacred festivals in honour of the motherland.[44]

To staff the national systems of education which they proposed, many of the reformers from the sixties onwards called for a new system of selecting and training teachers. Frequently they condemned reliance on religious orders. They argued that it was absurd to entrust training citizens to men whose primary loyalty was to their order rather than to the state, who had supposedly foresworn the things of this world, and who had chosen not to be fathers themselves. The abbé Pellicier, author of several memorials in 1763, was one of the first to call for a new corps of college teachers. He proposed special *maisons d'éducation* which would be subject to strict government control to ensure a uniform curriculum and a uniform methodology throughout France. The nation could not afford to allow teachers to pursue whatever goals they wished. "Toute éducation clandestine est suspecte, et par là-même, doit être réprouvée," he declared. "Le bien de la patrie demande que les Maîtres préposés au gouvernement d'un établissement public pour l'éducation,

41. Abbé Athanase Auger, *Discours sur l'éducation, prononcés au collège royal de Rouen* — Rouen, 1775, pp. 1-28. The preface to this work includes another "Esquisse d'un projet d'éducation nationale."

42. The appeal for military training combined with national indoctrination occurs repeatedly in the works by Thélis cited above.

43. Jean-Alexis Borrelly, *Plan de réformation des études* —, La Haye, 1776, p. 72.

44. Comte de Vauréal, *Plan ou essai d'éducation général et national, ou la meilleure éducation à donner aux hommes de toutes les nations*, Bouillon, 1783, v-viii.

n'ayent pas la liberté d'abonder dans leurs sens, pour donner à cet établissement telle forme, tel esprit qu'ils s'aviseront bon être."[45] Teachers would be trained to mould citizens useful to the motherland. Later Pellicier proposed similar training schools for elementary school teachers.[46] Others pleaded in vain for similar teachers' colleges down to the Revolution.

The hope of many educators was that they would not only inculcate citizens devoted to the motherland, but that they would develop individuals who would bring prestige to the nation. The objectives of college education are often revealed in notes in the programs of the *exercices publics*, at which students answered questions publicly, which many schools staged to impress parents, publicize the quality of their institution, and show off to local authorities. At such a ceremony at Le Mans an Oratorian professor told the audience that it was to produce men who would glorify the nation, that his school sought to develop the talents of youth. "Elle apporte, en naissant, des talens capables d'influer sur la gloire d'une Nation, et un coeur qui, sagement dirigé, devient un trésor pour la Société lorsqu'il est enflammé de l'amour du bien public, comme du sien propre."[47] Clearly the aim was not so much to enrich the life of the individual, but to produce the citizen who would distinguish his motherland.

Aulard, Hauser, and more recent historians have argued that the concept of *la patrie* could emerge fully only from the dissociation of the idea of the king from the idea of the nation. We have seen that patriotic devotion in the eighteenth century did tend to shift from the person of the king to the nation itself, but post-revolutionary historians have tended to exaggerate this dissociation and to date it too early. Many progressive thinkers of the Enlightenment did contend that there could be devotion to the motherland only in a community of free citizens living under

45. L'Abbé Pellicier, *Mémoires sur la nécessité de fonder une école pour former des maîtres, selon le plan d'éducation donné par le parlement en son arrêt du 3 septembre 1762*, Paris, 1763, III, p. 22.

46. [L'Abbé Pellicier] *Lettre à l'auteur des "Mémoires sur la nécessité de fonder une école pour former des maîtres"* —, s.l. 1763. Pellicier pretended to be one of his own readers. Here he advocates a school for schoolmasters. In his *Seconde lettre à l'auteur des Mémoires* he proposed a similar school for schoolmistresses.

47. Cited in Annette Bridgman, *History in the French Colleges in the Eighteenth Century*, Ph.D. dissertation, Queen's University, 1977, p. 227.

a government devoted to their welfare. However many of those who wished to engender national patriotism were unquestioning monarchists who continued to hope that the king would serve as the focal point of devotion to the motherland. What both groups shared was the belief that patriotism could only thrive where there was no despotism, where there were citizens rather than subjects, where they felt that the regime was devoted to their happiness, in short where they felt involved. That is what made education for citizenship vital to both groups. The hope expressed by Mathon that the king might lead a nation of patriots persisted into the early years of the Revolution. Only when the king failed to meet the test was he excised from the motherland.

The educational reform movement in prerevolutionary France, like so many reform efforts at the close of the *ancien régime*, was largely abortive, but this does not nullify its historical significance. First of all, it reminds us that the age of Enlightenment, which Peter Gay and others have seen primarily as an age when men threw off authority, when they affirmed their autonomy, was in fact also an age when many educators advocated rigid state control, mass indoctrination, and an homogenized citizenry. The reform movement in short emphasizes the ambiguous legacy of the philosophic century. There were trends toward individualism and nonconformity. Some eighteenth-century reformers did stress the need for a system of education which could provide for the peculiar nature of each child, but it would indeed have been surprising if most reformers had emphasized the need to encourage individual differences. As Lockians most of them believed that children were born without inherited differences. Children were identical blank slates, lumps of clay, or pieces of wax, ready to receive impressions from the legislator-educator. Reformers consequently thought it would be easy to impose the unity of outlook which they thought would strengthen the nation state.

Secondly, the educational reformers bequeathed certain notions some of which the revolutionaries, Napoleon, and even the politicians of the Third Republic attempted to put into practice. Some historians have objected that this continuity needs to be demonstrated in detail, presumably by proving that later educators read the prerevolutionary reformers. In my opinion such a demand reveals a naive approach to the history of ideas. Some ideas become so diffused that they become familiar clichés.

They are in the air so-to-speak. Lots of people use Freudian notions without ever having read Freud. When leaders in the Year II called for national public education, mass in-doctrination, and standardized textbooks they were echoing their predecessors before 1789. When Napoleon created a ministry of education, set up a highly centralized system of secondary schools, and imposed on all of France a common catechism inculcating loyalty to the ruler, he revealed himself a man of the eighteenth century. And was the centralized public school system which Jules Ferry and other republicans created later in the nineteenth century not part of the same legacy?

Finally, the largely abortive campaign for educational reform in the half century before the Revolution contributes to our judgement about that controversial question concerning the modernity of the eighteenth century. It seems that the would-be reformers raised all the fundamental issues about modern education — to what degree subjects should be relevant to current social needs, to what level various sections of the population should be schooled, to what extent women in par-ticular should be educated, what part science should play in the curriculum, how ethics should be treated in the schools, and what role the state ought to play in moulding future citizens. Obviously, all these questions concern us still.

James Leith

The Education of Princes:
Queen Anne and Her Contemporaries

Biographers of leading figures of the late seventeenth and early eighteenth centuries are confronted by a paucity of evidence concerning the early and formative years of their subjects. During the research for my forthcoming biography of Queen Anne I discovered that this state of affairs applies even to individuals of royal birth, whose lives by the nature of things are likely to be chronicled in more detail than those of lesser mortals. In part, the biographer is forced to rely upon inference and deduction in assessing his subject's scholastic experience; in many cases, one must rely upon contemporary biographies written years after the events being described and which may, or may not, be accurate. Given these difficulties, it is not surprising that the education of princes has been a topic largely ignored by modern historians. The only comparative effort which has come to my attention for the post-Renaissance period is *The Education of the Enlightened Despots,* ironically by a genuine Prince of Siam, which examines the early years of Louis XV, Frederick the Great, Catherine the Great, and Joseph II.[1] The result is four "mini-biographies," which fail to draw general conclusions. A survey of the education of princes of the previous generation — of Queen Anne and her contemporaries for the period 1660 to 1720 — allows the historian to establish a general pattern for royal training in the late seventeenth and early eighteenth centuries.

Education in the twentieth century is commonly defined in narrow terms of academic accomplishment, but for any understanding of royalty of the late seventeenth century, education must be defined in the broadest sense of the term — the prince's experiences from infancy through adolescence. Apart from theoretical considerations, it is a practical impossibility to emphasize academic achievement, for the most notable fact of

---

1. H.R.H. Prince Chula Chakrabongse of Siam, *The Education of the Enlightened Despots: A Review of the Youth of Louis XV of France, Frederick II of Prussia, Joseph II of Austria, and Catherine II of Russia* (London, 1948).

the seventeenth century was the widespread decline in educational standards from those of the Renaissance. No seventeenth century prince could match such Tudor prodigies as Elizabeth, Mary, and Edward VI, or Lady Jane Grey, in terms of academic achievement. Even in linguistic, historical, philosophical and theological training, the children of Ferdinand and Isabella, as exemplified by Catherine of Aragon, far outstripped the training of all but a handful of royal children two centuries later.[2]

This decline in educational standards was due in part to the widespread political upheavals of a century of ideological warfare produced by the Reformation. *Mittel Europa* was shattered politically and economically by the Thirty Years War. France underwent a century of instability ranging from the Wars of Religion in the sixteenth century through the assassination of Henri IV in 1610 to the rebellions of the nobility under Louis XIII and the Fronde, which so profoundly marred the adolescence of Louis XIV. From the First Bishops' War to the Restoration, the British Isles were convulsed by two decades of upheaval and continuous warfare. Consequently, it is fruitless to look for systematic and sustained plans of education for princes in the generation immediately preceding that of Queen Anne. The fact that Thomas Hobbes was Charles II's mathematics tutor during the first Stuart exile bears a great deal of relevance to Hobbes' political philosophy, but almost none to Charles II's interest or accomplishment in mathematics.

The long-term effects of this crisis of Europe were even more important than their immediate impact: by 1660 the struggle between Protestantism and Roman Catholicism had fatally wounded, if not killed outright, the Renaissance conception of the perfectibility of princes. By contrast to the copious literature of the fifteenth and sixteenth centuries on this theme, almost nothing on the education of princes saw print in the seventeenth century. The last major work on the subject was James VI and I's *Basilicon Doron,* published in 1603, an analysis of the King's own experiences as the basis of a program of education for his eldest son, Prince Henry. By the Restoration, however, *Basilicon Doron* had been widely discredited, both as a work of history and as an

2. Garrett Mattingly, *Catherine of Aragon* (New York, Vintage Books, 1960), pp. 3-28.

educational manual.[3] Early in his personal reign, Louis XIV adopted the same method for his famous *Mémoires* (which were published only in the early nineteenth century).[4] Although ostensibly devoted to the education of the dauphin, Louis's *Mémoires* bear closer resemblance to an autobiography than to an educational treatise. In any event, the fact that the Sun King abandoned the *Mémoires* after 1670, when he was only thirty-three and the dauphin only nine, suggests that Louis decided that they would serve no immediately useful purpose. In the majority of cases between 1660 and 1720, there was no single figure to map out an educational program for princes. It would remain to the nineteenth century to produce a Baron von Stockmar to lay down for Victoria and Albert a systematic program for the education of their son and heir, a program which proved a dismal failure in most of the desired objectives.[5] In the late seventeenth and early eighteenth centuries, decades before Jeremy Bentham defined it as a philosophical approach, utilitarianism was the method adopted by European monarchs in the education of their off-spring.

In this ultilitarian approach, the royal child was, above all, a Child of State and political considerations transcended all others, including parental rights and the emotional well-being of the child. The final source of authority in determining the child's future was the monarch, oftentimes without reference to the child's parents. Louis XIV dominated the education of his grandsons as surely as Charles II shaped the education of his nieces, Lady Mary and Lady Anne, just as George I prescribed the policies to be followed in rearing his grandchildren. It was not uncommon, albeit extreme, for political considerations to demand that a royal child be temporarily or permanently separated from his parents, even at tender years. At the age of ten, Queen Christina was removed permanently from the guardianship of her widowed and politically incompetent mother;[6] in 1679, at the height of the Popish Plot, when Charles

3. James Craigie, ed. *The Basilicon Doron of King James VI* (Scottish Texts Society, Edinburgh, 1944, 1950), II, 49-56.

4. For the publishing history of Louis XIV's *Mémoires*, see Paul Sonnino's translation (New York, 1970), p. 18.

5. For Stockmar's plan, see Philip Magnus, *King Edward the Seventh: The Most Edwardian of Them All* (London, Penguin edition, 1967), pp. 16-42.

6. Georgina Masson, *Queen Christina* (London, 1968), pp. 49-50.

II felt forced to send his Roman Catholic brother, James, Duke of York, and his wife, Mary of Modena, into exile in the Spanish Netherlands, he refused to let their daughters, Lady Anne (aged fourteen) and Lady Isabella (aged four), accompany them; the same ban applied when the Duke and Duchess transferred their exile to Scotland in 1680 and Lady Isabella died at St. James's in the absence of her parents.[7] The most extreme case was that of George I and his grandchildren, especially Prince Frederick Louis of Hanover. At the Elector of Hanover's accession to the British throne in 1714 as George I, when his grandson was seven, the King ordered that Frederick Louis should remain in Hanover to be reared as a German prince while Frederick's parents, the new Prince and Princess of Wales, should reside in London. This was the first indication that George I envisoned what later became his policy, the permanent separation of Great Britain and Hanover.[8] The principal result of this policy, aborted by George II on his father's death, was that Frederick Louis did not see his parents for over fourteen years. When the subterranean quarrel between George I and his son became a matter of public knowledge and partisan political exploitation in 1717 and the Prince and Princess of Wales were expelled from the royal palaces, the King ordered that his granddaughters should remain at Kensington under his direct, personal control. The Prince and Princess were allowed to visit their children in formal audience only on specially approved occasions.[9]

A favourite charge of Jacobite historians was that the participation of Princess Mary and Princess Anne in the 1688 revolution against their father, James II, was "unnatural", but

7. *Historical Manuscripts Commission* (HMC), *Ormonde* (new series) IV, 497-98, Sir Robert Southwell to the Duke of Ormonde, 8 March 1679 [London]; cf. Agnes Strickland, *Lives of the Queens of England* (London, 1851) VI, 83.

8. R. Drögereit, 'Das Testament König Georgs I und die Frage der Personalunion zwischen England und Hannover', *Niedersächsisches Jahrbuch für Landesgeschichte* (Hannover, 1937), 94-199, which is amplified by his English version, 'The Testament of King George I and the Problem of the Personal Union between England and Hanover', *Research and Progress*, V (1939); cf. R.M. Hatton, "In Search of an Elusive Ruler: Source material for a biography of George I as elector and King," *Fürst, Bürger, Mensch: Untersuchungen zu politischen and sozio-kulturellen Wandlungsprozessen im vorrevolutionären Europa*, ed. Friedrich Engel-Janosi (Wien, 1975), pp. 40-41.

9. John M. Beattie, *The English Court in the Reign of George I* (Cambridge, 1967), 271.

these propagandists missed the point. From the first moment of life political considerations transcended all other formative experiences in the training of a child of state. It was as natural for Mary and Anne to desert their father for political and religious reasons as it was for Queen Christina to ignore completely her mother as a political liability or for William III to disdain his paternal grandmother (his closest living relative) for having alienated the States-General, thereby endangering his political position in the Dutch Republic, by her political meddling during his minority.[10] The famous lifelong battle between Frederick, Prince of Wales, and his parents, George II and Queen Caroline, was politically motivated and was unique only in the violent personal antipathy felt on both sides.

Political considerations in part demanded that royal children be reared in both physical and emotional isolation. Parental disinterest in their children on a day-to-day basis seems astonishingly high by the bourgeois standards of the nineteenth and twentieth centuries. In part, this was a self-protective defense mechanism against the extraordinarily high rates of infant mortality in the late seventeenth century. The maternal misadventures of Queen Anne (who invariably referred to her children as 'my poor girl' or 'my poor boy', rather than any more specific name), with her seventeen pregnancies and eighteen children (only five of whom were born alive, two dying immediately after childbirth, two before their second birthdays and one — William, Duke of Gloucester — immediately after his eleventh birthday) are the best known. However, of the eighteen children born to James II's two wives, only four reached adolesence, while only one of Louis XIV's seven legitimate children reached maturity. (Bastards had better track records). In part, royal parental disinterest reflected an attitude which became general with the Victorian aristocracy: they were 'Olympian beings who must at all costs be protected from noise, intrusion, worry, interruption — in fact from children, in whom all such hazards are inherent'.[11]

From the moment of birth, therefore, the royal child was placed in the hands of a separate establishment or household

10. Masson, pp. 61-63; Stephen Baxter, *William III* (London, 1966), p. 41.
11. Violet Bonham Carter, *Winston Churchill as I Knew Him* (London, Pan Books, 1965), p. 25.

which undertook the most basic parental functions and, in the terminology of the age, became known as "the family". In the summer following Queen Anne's accession, Mrs. Martha Farthing claimed and received a £300 pension for having been 'wett nurse and did give sucke to her present Majestie Queene Anne for the space of fifteene monthes or thereabouts'.[12] Mrs. Farthing's daughter, Margery, roughly the same age as the future Queen and who was habitually referred to as the Queen's "foster sister",[13] served in her household throughout her life, despite the suspicion that Margery, 'a waspish ill natured creature', acted as a spy upon her mistress during the reign of William and Mary.[14]

"The Family" was invariably presided over by a governor and governess, who more often than not were husband and wife. In some cases, the appointment was traditional: in Scotland, the Earls of Mar were traditionally responsible for the welfare of royal infants. In some cases, monarchs relied on the hereditary principle in choosing those to preside over royal nurseries; the governor of Louis XIV was the Marquis de Villeroy and seventy years later, the aging king selected Villeroy's son to exercise control over the person of the future Louis XV. Sometimes members of "the Family" cared for two or more generations of royal infants: Bridget Holmes, the nurse of the children of Charles I, also administered to his grandchildren and Mrs. Beata Danvers, daughter of the poverty-stricken seventh Baron Chandos, entered the service of Anne Hyde, Duchess of York, and remained in the royal household until the death of Anne Hyde's daughter, Queen Anne.[15]

Obviously, proximity to royal children in their households could pay tremendous political dividends in the future: the most notable beneficiaries of this proximity were the son and four

12. Thurstan Peter, "Queen Anne's Nurse," *Notes and Queries*, series 11, V, 508.

13. James J. Cartwright, ed. *The Wentworth Papers, 1705-1739* (London, 1883), p. 282; Peter Wentworth to Lord Strafford, 28 March 1712, London; cf. Public Record Office, Treasury 48/23, n.f.: Sarah, Duchess of Marlborough, to William Lowndes, 2 August 1721, Windsor Lodge.

14. W.E. Buckley, ed. *Memoirs of Thomas, Earl of Ailesbury, written by Himself* (Roxburghe Club, London, 1890), p. 296.

15. For Bridget Holmes, see Oliver Millar, *The Tudor, Stuart, and Early Georgian Pictures in the Collection of Her Majesty the Queen* (London, 1963), I, 140; for Beata Danvers, see David Green, *Queen Anne* (London, 1970), p. 17.

daughters of Sir Edward and Lady Frances Villiers, the governor and governess of the children of James, Duke of York. The eldest daughter, Barbara, Lady Fitzharding, became a close companion of Princess Anne, while another daughter, Elizabeth Villers, later Countess of Orkney, accompanied Princess Mary to The Hague on her marriage and became *maitresse en titre* to William III. Their brother, Edward, was later created Earl of Jersey and given high diplomatic and political appointments, less in tribute to his own ability or political influence than to the fact that he had grown up with the last Stuart queens.

This future political potential of "the Family" was compounded by the physical isolation, in which royal children lived from the Court. In England, Richmond Palace was the traditional site for the households of royal children from the reign of Henry VII. The fact that William and Mary, after the Glorious Revolution, awarded the reversion of Richmond to yet another Villers sister rather than to Princess Anne's children was one of the principal bones of contention which later led to the famous quarrel between the Queen and Princess. Anne was forced to lease suburban Campden House, near Kensington Palace, for the household of her son, the Duke of Gloucester, although the Prince and Princess of Denmark and their own entourage remained permanently situated in central London, whether at the Cockpit, Berkeley House, or St. James's. In other courts, where the childrens' household remained within the precincts of the royal palace, this isolation was no less complete. In 1696, the exiled James II, at his court of St. Germain-en-Laye, drew up a list of 'Rules for the family of our dearest son, the Prince of Wales'. Among other provisions, the governor and the undergovernor were ordered to remain with the Prince at all times, 'none are to be permitted to whisper in the Prince his ear or talk with him in privat, out of the hearing of the Governor', and 'no children must be permitted to come into the Prince his lodgings, upon the account of playing with him, but when they are sent for, by the Governor . . . and not above two or three at a time.'[16] In light of this isolation and the future political potential for anyone lucky enough to grow up with a prince, the competition for a place in "the Family" was naturally fierce. The

16. *HMC Stuart* I, 114-17: 'Rules for the family of our dearest son, the Prince of Wales' [by James II], 19 July 1696, St. Germain.

final determination, of course, was made by the monarch. In 1713, Hans Caspar von Bothmer, the Hanoverian envoy to London, suggested that one of the sons of the Duke of St. Albans should be placed in the household of Prince Frederick Louis, both because of the child's royal blood (St. Albans was Charles II's bastard by Nell Gwyn) and because he would help the Hanoverian prince learn to speak English. The Elector, however, rejected this proposal, ostensibly because of St. Albans' close identification with the Whig party but also undoubtedly because of the Elector's plan to rear his eldest grandson as a German prince.[17] In establishing the composition of a royal household, even a royal command could be evaded by a bold and ambitious woman, bent upon blatant nepotism. In 1698, when the Duke of Gloucester was given an independent establishment under the supervision of John Churchill, Earl of Marlborough, Princess Anne's closest friend, Lady Marlborough, was intent upon securing an appointment for her young cousin, John Hill (the brother of Sarah's future nemesis, Abigail Masham. As Sarah recalled five years later:

> Mr. Hill, who had served the Prince many years as a Page, & grown too big for it, the Princess designed to provide for him in the Duke of Gloucester's Bedchamber: But forseeing that the King would strike out any body who had nothing to support them but their Service to the Prince or Princess, prevailed with my Lord Marlborough to leave him out of the List which he gave my Lord Albemarle, resolving to add him after the List came back, it being reasonable to have more than two Grooms of the Bedchamber, who were to run after a Child from morning to night.
>
> I thought the Princess might add him after all the others were fix'd, & that it was impossible at the King's Return [i.e., from The Hague] for Him to turn him out. This Stratagem succeeded so well, that I am not sure whether the King ever knew Mr. Hill was Groom of the Bedchamber.[18]

As Sarah's comment implied, among other functions, the

17. Niedersäsisches Staatsarchiv [NSA], Hannover: Hannover 92, III A, No. 12 III, f. 61: Jean de Robethon to Hans Caspar von Bothmer, 17 August 1713.

18. Blenheim G I 9: Mss. copy [1703] of Sarah's "Conduct," f. 12. I am

household was to provide the necessary discipline for a prince, but even such guidance oftentimes had a political flavour. In 1708, Mrs. Ruperta Howe, wife of the English envoy at Hanover, described to the Duchess of Marlborough the unique situation at the Hanoverian court, where there were four generations (the dowager Electress Sophia, the Elector, the Electoral Prince and Princess, and Prince Frederick Louis) and the bizarre behaviour of the latter:

> I can not help obsearving what imprestions may be put into a child of a year and five months old who was taught to fly at his great Grandmother like a little Tyger and tare her black whoods, to flatter and kiss his Grandfather's hand, to be kind to them that are in favour and looke like a fury uppon those that are not, if I had not seen this I should not beleive it possible.[19]

Childhood isolation provided the royal child with ample opportunity for the close observation of servants, to determine whether they were honest, trustworthy, and efficient. It also bred distrust and cynicism, and a pronounced proclivity to indulge in backstairs political intrigue. In some princes, such as George II, childhood isolation produced an exaggerated sociability, but in the majority of cases, it produced an adult desire for privacy, not to say outright anti-social behavior. One major reason for William III's unpopularity with the English aristocracy was his pronounced unwillingness to carouse with his nobles as his uncle, Charles II, had been only too willing to do. Physical invalidism, combined with an intense desire for a private life shared with only a handfull of intimates, made Queen Anne a virtual recluse. George I, as Elector and King, shunned ceremonial and large social gatherings, leaving social responsibilities to his son and daughter-in-law until 1717, when the establishment of a rival court at Leicester House made it politically necessary for the King to enter the social lists.[20] Even Louis XIV, who adapted and perfected the Habsburg court ceremonial of his great-grandfather, Philip II, in which the King was on public display

---

grateful to His Grace, the Duke of Marlborough, for permission to quote from the manuscripts in the Blenheim muniment room.

19. Blenheim E 44: Mrs. Ruperta Howe to Sarah, 2-13 July [1708], Hanover.

20. Beattie, passim.

from his *levée* to his *couchée,* soon came to regard himself as the prisoner of his own creation. In later years, Louis jealously guarded his hours of privacy and domesticity in the suites of Madame de Maintenon (where, according to a spy, the King waited on his morganatic wife 'in almost bourgeois fashion. Then she goes to bed while the King chats to her, et Souvent fait apporter par une de ses femmes une chaise percée, et pousse une selle auprès de son lit'.)[21] In addition, Louis found occasional afternoons of escape at the Grand Trianon within the grounds of Versailles and — most importantly — his frequent expeditions to the completely separate chateau at Marly, where he could entertain a few favoured intimates *en bourgeois.* At the age of seven or eight, a prime was formally removed from the care of nurses and governesses and placed in 'men's hands' which also marked the beginning of the double standard in education, as princesses generally remained within the confines of the nursery). This entailed the appointment of a new governor, generally a nobleman of high political or military importance.; henceforth, the governor was to manage "the Family", which was usually greatly expanded at this point, and to provide discipline and an example to his charge. When William III appointed Marlborough as Gloucester's governor in 1698, he told him, 'Make my nephew learn what you are, and he shall not lack accomplishments.' In addition, a preceptor or tutor — usually a high-ranking clergyman — was appointed to supervise a number of subordinates in the academic education of the prince. Both the governor and the preceptor obviously had ample scope to develop future political influence with their charges. Both the Duc de Beauvilliers and François de Salignac de la Mothe-Fenelon, Archbishop of Cambrai, the governor and preceptor respectively of Louis XIV's eldest grandson, the duc de Bourgogne, retained their guiding position with that prince until his untimely death in 1712.[22] The most famous example of future influence was that of the tutor of Louis XIV's nephew, the future Regent, Philippe, duc d'Orléans: despite the hostility of

21. Winston S. Churchill, *Marlborough, His Life and Times* (London, 1947), II, 584, quoting a letter from an unidentified agent at Versailles, 5 August 1709.

22. John C. Rule, "King and Minister: Louis XIV and Colbert de Torcy," *William III and Louis XIV,* ed. R.M. Hatton and J.S. Bromley (Liverpool, 1968), p. 220.

Orléans' parents (especially his mother), his political associates, and eventually Louis XIV himself, Guillaume Dubois gained a transcendent influence over Orleans, eventually becoming Secretary of State for Foreign Affairs and principal minister, a Cardinal of the Roman Catholic Church, and the political mastermind of the Regency until his death a few months before that of his former pupil.[23] In other cases, however, the relationship between teacher and pupil proved to be less happy. Frederick, Prince of Wales' tutor, Monsieur Neibourg, informed Queen Caroline of her son that 'His was the most vicious nature, and the most false heart that ever man had, nor are his vices the vices of a gentleman'.[24] This intensity of feeling was undoubtedly due, in large measure, to the fact that the tutor and pupil worked closely together on a one-on-one basis; of the princes of this period, only William III enjoyed anything approaching a modern education, and the lectures which he attended at the University of Leyden were prepared especially for him.[25]

The invariable appointment of a clergyman as preceptor underlined the central importance of religion in the training of princes. Indeed, religion retained its medieval importance as the central focus of education. While younger sons were no longer destined for a priestly life, in those areas of Europe most deeply influenced by the evangelical zeal of the Counter-Reformation, princesses often prepared to enter a religious order. Mary of Modena was so devoted to the prospect of becoming a nun that only orders from the Pope himself that she would do greater work for God by marrying James, Duke of York, and participating in the restoration of the True Faith in three kingdoms sufficed to alter her decision to sacrifice celibacy for a missionary career.[26] Dowager queens of Spain could expect to spend their years of widowhood in a convent, an appalling prospect which induced Philip V's second wife, Elizabeth Farnese, to embark on a policy

23. The most complete studies of the relationship between Orléans and Dubois remain those by Louis Wiesener, *Le Régent, l'Abbé Dubois et les Anglais*, 3 vols. (Paris, 1891-1899), and Emile Bourgeois, *La Diplomatie Secrète du XVIIIe Siècle*, I: *Le Secret du Régent et La Politique de L'Abbé Dubois* (Paris, 1907).
24. Morris Marples, *Poor Fred & The Butcher, Sons of George II* (London, 1970), pp. 6-7.
25. Baxter, p. 23.
26. Martin Haile, *Queen Mary of Modena, Her Life and Letters* (London, 1905), pp. 20-22.

of obtaining for her own son, Don Carlos, a separate Kingdom where his widowed mother might find a refuge; in the process, the Farnese upset the diplomatic structure of Europe.[27]

In most European courts, however, both princes and princesses were destined to fulfill a lay, dynastic role. Consequently, evangelicalism was soft-pedalled in religious training in favour of traditional, conservative, and unquestioning approaches to doctrinal questions. Rarely was the preceptor suspect from deviation from orthodoxy. In 1704, when James III's tutors were accused of Jansenist sympathies, the subsequent investigation caused a terrible uproar, involving not only the Court of St. Germain, but also Cardinal Noailles as Archbishop of Paris, and Madame de Maintenon.[28] Generally, however, the product of princely religious training tended to be quietly and genuinely devoted to the religion of his youth, although he was generally able to make political compromises when necessary. After 1688, William III remained a Calvinist at heart, as George I remained a Lutheran after 1714, although both monarchs publicly conformed to the ceremonial and liturgy of the Church of England, of which they were Heads. Only rarely did religious scruple overcome political necessity, for they usually marched hand in hand: the outright refusal of the Pretender in early 1714 to convert to Protestantism, thereby enabling Oxford and Bolingbroke, the ministers of his half-sister, Queen Anne, to overthrow the Act of Settlement and the Hanoverian Succession, was out of tune with the standards of the age.[29]

Part of the prince's religious training, of course, was devoted to explaining the doctrines of the national church, but a larger part and a greater effort was devoted to exposing the fallacies of rival heresies. The result was that princes, in a quiet way, tended

27. Bourgeois, II: *Le Secret des Farnèse, Philippe V, et la Politique d'Alberoni* (Paris, 1909), passim.

28. *HMC Stuart* I, 188-93, documents the charges of Jansenism. For the broad connections between the Jacobites in exile and the Jansenist community, see Ruth Clark, *Strangers and sojourners at Port Royal, being an account of the connections between the British Isles and the Jansenists of France and Holland* (Cambridge, 1932).

29. The account of J.H. and Margaret Shennan, "The Protestant Succession, April 1713 - September 1715," *William III and Louis XIV*, ed. Hatton and Bromley, should be supplemented by G. Edward Gregg, "The Protestant Succession in International Relations, 1710-1716," unpublished London Ph.D. thesis, 1972.

to harbour prejudices verging on bigotry. In 1679, the adolescent Lady Anne, visiting the Spanish Netherlands, was struck by the Roman Catholic 'images which are in every shope & corner of the street, the more I heare of that Religion, the more I dislike it'.[30] In the last year of her life, she feared to place her trust in a foreign diplomat 'because he was a Roman Catholic',[31] As a result of this negative emphasis, moral training in the broadest sense tended to get short shrift. Fenelon's high principles — and even more the duc de Bourgogne's attempts to live up to them — stand out as rarities during the period.

Religious training also served as the basis for an explanation of recent history. Ideology and propaganda marched hand in hand through the royal nursery. For instance, in the immediate aftermath of the Restoration, the English granddaughters of Charles I were taught to regard him as the Martyr King who had died in defense of the Church of England. In her ultimately unsuccessful struggle to convince Queen Anne of the merits of the Whig party, Sarah, Duchess of Marlborough, repeatedly complained that she was confronted by two insuperable obstacles: first, the "priests" — as Sarah scathingly referred to them, had thoroughly propagandized their royal charge as a child, equating Puritan rebels with the modern Whigs; second, monarchs were unaccustomed to hearing the truth. In November, 1704, as part of her campaign, Sarah wrote the Queen a letter, in one paragraph of which Sarah managed to impugn the Queen's education, her intelligence, and her grandparents:

> I find plainly, that Mrs. Morley [the Queen] & her faithfull Freeman [Sarah] differs only in the name, I believe she has sucked in with her milk a great abhorance of what they call'd in those days Whigs, or round heads, I don't at all wonder at it, I will allow they had cloven feet, or what you please, tho there is nothing more certain, then that you never heard the whole truth of that story [i.e., the English civil war], there being few that will venture to displease one

30. Lt. Col, the Hon. Benjamin Bathurst, ed. *Letters of Two Queens* (London, 1924), 108-9: Lady Anne to Frances Apsley, 22 September, [1679], Brussels.

31. Philip Roberts, ed. *The Diary of Sir David Hamilton, 1709-1714* (Oxford, 1975), p. 66, quoting Queen Anne.

they hope to have their fortunes made by, & don't care to be so singular as to tell you tis possible you may be misinform'd, but I that have read every booke little & greate, that has been writ upon that subject, can assure you the extream weakness of that unfortunate King [Charles I] contribute as much to his misfortunes, as all the malice of those ill men, nay I will venture to say more, that it had not been possible for them to have hurt him, if he had not been govern'd by almost as bad people, without knowing it, the Queen Mother [Henrietta Maria] who had absolute power over him, not being only a french woman (which was misfortune enough) but a very ill woman . . .[32]

By contrast to religion as a vehicle for the study of recent history, the study of the humanities and social sciences in a formal academic sense tended to be underplayed. In his instructions concerning the Prince of Wales, James II referred simply to his son 'doing his book'. Following the utilitarian approach, linguistic training received the greatest emphasis, although royal students rarely achieved a high level of expertise. Training in French was universal, while most males mastered enough rudimentary Latin to read international treaties. William III, the greatest linguist of the period, in addition to Latin was orally proficient in Dutch, German, English, and Spanish; French was William's language of preference, but his letters are replete with grammatical and spelling errors. The Pretender, trained in English, French, and Italian, remained charmingly idyosyncratic in his usage of each language, while his handwriting remains the despair of historians. Both Queen Mary and Queen Anne remained on unsure territory throughout their lifelong struggles with the intricacies of English grammar and syntax, although both could occasionally deploy the language with surprising warmth and elegance. George I and George II were required by political necessity to learn English as adults, the one to a lesser,[33] the other to a greater degree. In general, practical considerations determined the extent and degree of a prince's linguistic accomplishments.

---

32. Blenheim G I 7: Sarah to the Queen, 20 Nov. 1704, Windsor Park.

33. For George I's command of English, see R.M. Hatton, "In Search of an Elusive Ruler," cited in 8. There is evidence that the Elector secretly began to study English soon after the passage of the Act of Settlement (John Toland, *An*

In most cases, we possess few if any records of the formal training of princes in history or geography. It is a safe assumption, however, that these subjects were pursued with an eye to the national or dynastic interests of the prince's family. In some cases, study in the humanities became self-education as an adult. Both the Electress Sophia and Princess Caroline discussed and studied philosophy under the guidance of Leibniz. Queen Anne obviously studied the reign of Elizabeth intensely. In 1692, during her dispute with William and Mary, Princess Anne drew a comparison between her own position and that of Elizabeth under Mary Tudor.[34] In 1702, the new Queen adopted Elizabeth's motto, patterned her coronation robes on Elizabeth's, and resurrected the Elizabethan custom of Thanksgiving services at St. Paul's Cathedral.

In one famous case, we have the record left by a boastful tutor of the academic regime to which his charge was subjected. In his *History of My Own Time,* Gilbert Burnet, Bishop of Salisbury, recorded of his pupil, the Duke of Gloucester:

> I had been trusted with his education now for two years; and he had made an amazing progress. I had read over the Psalms, Proverbs, and Gospels with him, and had explained things that fell in my way, very copiously; and was often surprised with the questions that he put me, and the relections that he made. He came to understand things relating to religion, beyond imagination. I went through geography so often with him, that he knew all the maps very particularly. I explained to him the forms of government in every country, with the interests and trade of that country, and what was both good and bad in it; I acquainted him with all the great revolutions that had been in the world and gave him a copious account of the Greek and Roman histories, and of Plutarch's lives; the last thing I explained

Account of the Courts of Prussia and Hanover [London, 1705], pp. 71-72) and that he knew a great deal more of the language than he ever admitted publicly. In 1707, Sir Rowland Gwynne, who spent three years at the Hanoverian court, apparently believed that the Elector spoke English: "I allsoe beg pardon for writeing in English, which I hope will be the more easily granted, since I believe that your Electoral Highness is master of the language;" British Museum, Stowe 223, ff. 25-29: Gwynne to Elector, 2 April 1707, Hamburg.

34. HMC Finch IV, 452-53: [Dr. Richard Kingston to Nottingham], c. 11 September 1692.

to him was the Gothic constitution, and the beneficiary and feudal laws: I talked of these things at different times, near three hours a day: this was both easy and delighting to him. The King ordered five of his chief ministers to come once a quarter, and examine the progress he made: they seemed amazed both at his knowledge, and the good understanding that appeared in him; he had a wonderful memory, and a very good judgment.[35]

Academic training in history and geography was all the more important, as the Grand Tour was definitely limited for seventeenth century princes. Apart from Peter the Great's famous travels, few princes visited countries other than their own, although in 1669-1670, Prince George of Denmark visited Paris and London,[36] and in 1678-1680, Georg Ludwig of Hanover supplemented his previous trips to Italy with visits to France and England.[37]

Training in the arts was based on practical rather than aesthetic considerations. Every "family" had a dancing master, as dancing was the second most important social activity at seventeenth and eighteenth century courts. (Gambling was the first and in the case of most princes, their training here was less systematic and successful here than in any other field). Drama was taught on the basis of participation rather than appreciation. Theatrical and musical presentations of Louis XIV's reign, often involving members of the royal family, are famous. In 1674, the diarist John Evelyn attended a performance of *Calisto, or the Chaste Nymphe* at the Palace of Whitehall: the King, Queen, Duke and Duchess of York, and the entire Court were in attendance to see Lady Mary (aged twelve) and Lady Anne (aged nine), 'all covered with jewels', acting in minor roles.[38] The results of such practical training varied: Queen

35. Gilbert Burnet, *History of My Own Time* (London, 1832), IV, 451-52.
36. For notices of Prince George of Denmark's Grand Tour, see PRO, SP 101/15, f. 326: Newsletter, 18 September 1668, Paris; SP 101/16, f. 52: Newsletter 19 April 1669, Paris; *Calendar of State Papers, Venice* XXXVI, 90: Mocenigo to Doge & Senate, 16 August 1669, London: *HMC Le Fleming* 65: Newsletter, 20 July 1669, [London].
37. For Georg Ludwig's travels as a young man, see George Schnath, *Geschichte Hannovers im Zeitalter der neunten Kur und der englischen Sukzession, 1674-1714* (Hildesheim, 1938), 150-60.
38. E.S. de Beer, ed. *The Diary of John Evelyn* (Oxford, 1955), IV, 49-50,

Mary often attended the theatre, while Queen Anne had only four plays presented at Court in a three year period, preferring operatic concerts by Italian artists, as well as less elevated entertainment (her privy purse accounts record ten guineas paid 'to the Woman for Dancing the Doggs before the Queen'.)[39] Both princesses, on Charles II's initiative, received rhetorical training from Mrs. Barry, a noted actress of the Restoration stage, and the beauty and clearness of Queen Anne's voice was invariably commented upon by observers of her speeches to Parliament.[40] In terms of music, princesses were expected to master at least one instrument — usually a lute or harpsicord — although princes also received musical training. Louis XIV had a life-long love of, and well-developed appreciation for, music, while his nephew, Philippe, duc d'Orléans, became a composer of minor note. William III acted as a patron of Henry Purcell, while both George I and George II sponsored Handel.

In an age of growing elegance, surprisingly little emphasis was placed on formal training in the plastic arts, apart from the obligatory training of princesses in sewing and other domestic skills. The standards of the age were best expressed by Queen Anne, who preferred the portraiture of Michael Dahl to the more stylized productions of Sir Godfrey Kneller because Dahl's renditions were 'more like flesh & blood'.[41] Just as allegorical themes were increasingly based on political rather than religious subjects, royal patronage of the arts took on political significance. During her eleven years at The Hague, Mary of Orange developed a taste for Chinese export art; after 1689, when she brought her extensive collection of plates, vases, and bowls to decorate Kensington Palace, she was widely imitated and *chinoiserie* became a dominant theme of eighteenth century English interior decor.[42] William III established a notable collection of Old Masters at Het Loo, and the English politicians and soldiers in his entourage — notably Marlborough — quickly

entry for 15 December 1674.

39. John Ashton, *Social Life in the Reign of Queen Anne* (London 1897), 255: Edgar Sheppard, *Memorials of St. James's Palace* (London, 1894, I, 280-81; Hove Public Library, M 1/112/5; Privy purse accounts, 9 January 1710).

40. Burnet, V, 2: notes by Dartmouth and Onslow.

41. Blenheim E 17: Princess Anne to Lady Marlborough, Fryday night [c. October 1692], Campden House.

42. Elizabeth Hamilton, *William's Mary* (London, 1972), pp. 258-61.

followed suit. The longtime connection of the Hanoverian court with Italy and the extensive Hanoverian collections of classical antiquities reinforced, in the early eighteenth century, a contest within the English aristocracy to accent new country palaces with classical Italian artifacts. The greatest royal collector of the period was the duc d'Orléans, who made his Paris home, the Palais Royal, one of the finest museums in France with his acquisitions from Spain during his military service there and through his purchase of the bulk of Queen Christina's famous collection.[43]

By contrast to the arts, the scientific revolution only slowly penetrated palaces. Scientific training of royal children was almost unknown. As an adult, Orléans won unique fame by studying chemistry (and also an unjustified reputation as a poisoner). Mathematics was studied principally because it was useful for military purposes.

Just as religion dominated the academic portion of a prince's education, military training dominated the practical aspects of his life. Training began as soon as the prince was able to mount a horse. David Nairne, the chief clerk for the foreign office of the court of St. Germain-en-Laye, proudly chronicled in his diary James III's progress from smaller to larger steeds.[44] The intense military training of Charles XII and Frederick the Great is too well known to require comment. William III's health was too delicate for him to participate in rigorous military training as a young boy and not until he was sixteen could he manage all the paraphenalia necessary. This weakness was a cause of grave concern, for his supporters feared that he would be unable to qualify for the office traditional in his family, Captain-General of the Dutch Republic.[45] Military training had an obvious political purpose: future monarchs were also future commanders-in-chief. Military training also had a more immediate and useful political and military purpose. Often a young prince was given a titular command in order to protect a commander of genius but of common birth, who in the absence of the prince's

43. The bulk of the Orleans collection, purchased by the Duke of Sutherland at the time of the French Revolution, is today on permanent loan to the National Gallery of Scotland.

44. National Library of Scotland, Acc. 4920: Sir David Nairne's journal, passim.

45. Baxter, pp. 36-37.

protection might be overruled by noblemen. Louis XIV used both his son and his eldest grandson to circumvent the class system for the benefit of the state.

Military training also contributed to the health and physical training of the prince, and led virtually every man of royal birth into the "sport of kings", hunting. With many royal figures, the hunt became an over-riding passion, not least because it offered a rare opportunity for privacy and freedom from importunity. This passion was not confined to men alone; even as an elderly lady, Louis XIV's sister-in-law and the Regent's mother, Elizabeth Charlotte, duchesse d'Orléans, loved to follow the hunt from her coach, while Queen Anne in the last years of her life hunted in Windsor Great Park in a small chariot with two horses.

Last, but certainly not least, one should not ignore the sexual education of princes; again, in the spirit of the age, this was characterized by practice rather than theory. The principal duty of princes was to propagate their dynasty, and for men this meant early sexual initiation. At the age of sixteen, Louis XIV was abruptly introduced to sexual contact by one of his mother's ladies in waiting, Madame de Beauvais;[46] James III, at the age of twenty, was relatively old when, according to a Hanoverian agent, 'une démoiselle d' Arras . . . a eu le Pucelage de ce Prince'.[47] The first mistress of Frederick of Hanover, Madame d'Elitz, had served in the same capacity to his father and grandfather.[48] Sometimes, when political purposes demanded, there might even be tacit encouragement of homosexual tendencies: Anne of Austria and Cardinal Mazarin, conscious of the political difficulties caused by Louis XIII's younger brother, Gaston d'Orleans, deliberately ignored the homosexual practices of Anne's younger son, Philippe, in the hope that this would render him less of a political threat to his elder brother, Louis XIV.[49] Princes who were carefully excluded from political life, such as Louis XIV's nephew, the future Regent, might turn to sexual excess for want of anything better to do.

46. John B. Wolf, Louis XIV (New York, 1968), p. 94.
47. NSA, Cal. Br. 24, Frankreich 182, ff. 96-97: [Martines] to Robethon, 10 August 1714, Paris.
48. Marples, p. 6; cf. John Walters, The Royal Griffin: Frederick, Prince of Wales, 1707-1751 (New York, 1972), pp. 32-33.
49. Philippe Erlanger, Monsieur, Frere de Louis XIV (Paris, 1953), pp. 36-42.

Subjected then to political considerations, for the princes of the late seventeenth and early eighteenth century, these became the paramount factors of their lives, even to the exclusion of normal human ties of family and friendship. Their educations tended to make them wary and suspicious of the motives of others, often to the point of cynicism. They placed high premiums on privacy and upon blind loyalty in others. In our enlightened age, we would regard them, more or less, as neurotics. The seventeenth century called them "unnatural". But no one can hope to understand Queen Anne and her royal contemporaries without appreciating the extraordinary system by which the royal houses of Europe educated their princes.

Edward Gregg

"I Never Learned Anything
at the Little Schools":
Pope's Roman Catholic
Education

Although it is extremely difficult to gather as much reliable information as one would want on this matter, a careful investigation of the available documents convinces one that Alexander Pope's Catholic education is an aspect of his life which has never been adequately examined. His acquaintance as a student with Catholics who were persecuted and prosecuted for their religious convictions has never been sufficiently stressed in any biographical treatment.

This essay will attempt first to set the record straight as to whom Pope studied with and when. Sections on three Catholic educators Pope studied with or is presumed to have studied with will follow. The general nature and organization of one of the schools the poet attended (presumably the other was similar) will be detailed. And finally, I shall offer some speculations on the type of language and moral instruction Pope probably received.

Pope's "extremely loose and disconcerted"[1] formal education is one of the greatest problems besetting any person interested in the poet's biography. Not only is there a paucity of reliable information, but even the presumed reliable information is open to question. The chronology must first be established. Pope told Spence in 1739 that his

first education was under a priest, and I think his name was Banister. He set out with the design of teaching him Latin and Greek together.

I was then about eight years old, had learnt to read of an old aunt, and to write by copying printed books. After

---

1. Joseph Spence in "Anecdotes by and about Alexander Pope," *Observations, Anecdotes, and Characters of Books and Men*, ed. James M. Osborn (Oxford, 1966), I. 9. Pope *1742*, Item 15. All citations from Spence are from the Osborn edition. In addition to page references, Spence's dating will be given together with the anecdote reference number.

having been under that priest about a year I was sent to the
seminary at Twyford. . . .[2]

Spence, always fascinated by the problem of the poet's early
education, constantly tried to draw information out of him on
the subject.

> He began for Latin and Greek together (which is the way in
> the schools of the Jesuits, and which he seemed to think a
> good way) under Banister, their family priest, who was
> living (says he) not above two years ago at Sir Harry
> Tichborne's. He then learned his accidence at Twyford
> where he wrote a satire on some faults of his master.[3]

> It was our family priest who taught me the figures, ac-
> cidence, and first part of the grammar. If it had not been
> for that, I should never have got any language, for I never
> learned anything at the little schools I was at after. . . .[4]

> Mr. Pope was taught his accidence and the Greek elements
> [the alphabet only] by a priest in the family, was sent to the
> school at Twyford when he was about eight. . . .[5]

It will be noted that the poet never contradicts the information
first given in 1739. Johnson in his *Lives of the Poets* is at variance
with the information Pope gave to Spence. He says that when
Pope was about eight years old,

> he was placed in Hampshire under Taverner, a Romish
> priest, who by a method very rarely practised taught him
> the Greek and Latin rudiments together . . . . From the
> care of Taverner, under whom his proficiency was con-
> siderable, he was removed to a school at Twyford. . . .[6]

This is the point at which difficulties begin for the modern
scholar. In 1696, Edward Taverner (alias John Banister and John

---

2. Spence, I. 8. Pope *June 1739,* Item 14.
3. Spence, I. 9. Pope *1742,* Item 15.
4. Spence, I. 10. Pope *March 1743,* Item 17.
5. Spence, I. 10. Pope *18-21 January 1743,* Item 18.
6. Samuel Johnson, *Lives of the Poets, A Selection,* ed. J. P. Hardy (Oxford,
1971), pp. 210-11. Johnson is not at all reliable for information on Pope's
schooling. "To Binfield Pope was called by his father when he was about twelve
years old, and there he had for a few months the assistance of one Deane,
another priest, of whom he learned only to construe a little of Tully's *Offices*".
(p. 211). Deane was not a priest, and Pope went to Binfield *after* his stay at
Deane's.

Davis) became master at Twyford. James M. Osborn, in his edition of Spence, remarks:

> The fact that Pope followed Banister, the family priest, to Twyford seems to explain why the poet's parents would have felt assurance in letting the child go far from home.[7]

There is, however, no real evidence that the Banister at Hampshire and the Banister at Twyford are the same person. There is even less to suggest that Taverner's tutelage began before Pope went to Twyford.

Pope himself on the four occasions quoted above did not identify the two Banisters as the same person. Pope's half-sister, Mrs. Rackett, told Spence, "We had always a priest in the house to teach him."[8] She also remarked that her brother "was whipped and ill-used at Twyford School for his satire on his master, and was taken from thence on that account."[9] It is strange that Mrs. Rackett did not identify the "priest in the house" with the master who "whipped and ill-used" her brother. The reverend Mr. Mannock, a family friend, similarly does not remark on the same person as being resident at both Hampshire and Twyford.[10] Perhaps the most conclusive piece of factual evidence is Pope's remark that Banister, the family priest who taught him, was living at Sir Harry Tichborne's about 1740. Other evidence concerning Banister, the Twyford master, states that he retired from that school in about 1726 and went to live with the Holmans, at Warkworth, near Banbury, where he died in August, 1745.[11]

There is a Benedictine tradition which gives the honor to a

7. Osborne's note to Item 14 (I. 8.)
8. Spence, I. 9. Mrs. R(ackett) 28 July-4 August 1738, Item 16.
9. Spence, 1. 10 Mrs. R(ackett) 28 July-4 August 1738, Item 20.
10. Spence, I. 10. Mannock 1-7 May 1739, Item 19.
11. Bernard Ward, *History of St. Edmund's College* (London, 1893), p. 8 gives the following account of Taverner: "Mr. Taverner ruled Twyford for many years, till well on in the eighteenth century. Eventually he removed to Warkworth Castle, the seat of the Holmans, who possessed property near Winchester, and were very probably amongst the school's principal benefactors and patrons. Here he died in 1745."

Robert W. Rogers in "Notes on Alexander Pope's Early Education," *The South Atlantic Quarterly*, Vol. LXX, No. 2 (Spring, 1971), 236-47 quotes "a most interesting entry [which] appears in the poll-tax list of 1692 in the Corporation of London Record Office (Assessment Box 32, MS. 5.). Noted as living in the parish of St. Edmund the King in Lombard Street precinct are Alexander

member of their congregation. John and Thomas Dancastle (the Thomas who was a close friend of Pope's) entered St. Gregory's school at Douay on June 11, 1682. On September 6 of that year a William Bannester joined the school. Bannester became a Benedictine, went to Bath in 1714, stayed there for the rest of his life, and ultimately became Provincial of Canterbury (the southern of the two Benedictine Provinces). In 1725 he was made titular Prior of Bath by General Chapter and was runner-up for the Presidency of the entire Congregation. He died at Bath on May 16, 1726.[12] Pope's recollection to Spence in 1742 (cited above) that "Banister, their family priest, . . . was living . . . not above two years ago at Sir Harry Tichborne's" indicates that the Benedictine tradition is inaccurate.

In 1696, Pope went to Twyford school where Edward Taverner alias Banister had just been appointed master. The nature of the satire against Taverner has never been revealed, but it has been noted that "some of Pope's verses were still to be seen scratched on the window at Twyford"[13] long after Pope's departure.

After his escapade at Twyford, Pope "was a little while at Mr. Deane's seminary at Marylebone, and some time under the same, after he removed to Hyde Park Corner."[14] Since Pope asserted that his institutional education ended at the age of twelve when he went to Binfield,[15] this means that Pope must have been under Deane's tutelage for approximately three years, between 1697 and 1700.

The Popes moved from London to Binfield not before 1698

Pope, merchant and wife (£1.4s.), and two servants, 'Mary Baron' . . . and 'John Taverner.' It appears possible that Taverner (i.e., Banister) may have enjoyed an association with the Pope family almost immediately after his return to England in 1692 (238). Rogers' article is an excellent outline of Pope's education, and he cites the 'Terms of Admission' at Twyford (see below).

12. There are two manuscript sources for this tradition: Rev. Athanasius Allanson, O.S.B. in *A History of the English Benedictine Congregation from its establishment by Paul V on the 23 August 1619 to the Restoration of the Hierarchy in England* — (c. 1850) and *Biographies of the English Benedictines* (c. 1850). Both these manuscript volumes are in the Archives of Ampleforth Abbey.

13. C. T. Wickham, *The Story of Twyford School* (Winchester, 1909), p. 6. The source for the recollection is the Rev. Latham Wickham who was the headmaster there from 1862-1887.

14. Spence, I. 9. Pope *1742*, Item 15.

15. Spence, I. 8. Pope *June 1739*, Item 14.

and not after 1701.[16] About that time, "[when] about twelve, [he] went with [his] father into the Forest and there learned for a few months under a fourth priest."[17] The identity of the "fourth priest" is difficult to uncover. He may have been William Mannock (1677-1749), mentioned above, who became family priest in the household of Charles Rackett, Pope's brother-in-law, about 1700, soon after his return from the English College at Rome. The Racketts lived at Hallgrove, Bagshot, only eight miles from Binfield, and Mannock would, perhaps, have had the opportunity of tutoring the young Pope.[18] However, this speculation seems unlikely at a closer glance. Mannock spoke with Spence in May of 1739. At no time did he indicate to Spence that he had been the poet's teacher. Since Pope's education was a matter of overwhelming interest to Spence, it seems likely that he would have questioned Mannock closely on that score.

Still another biographical problem regarding the education of Pope must be examined. Although Pope speaks of only two schoolmasters at educational institutions (presumably Taverner and Deane), there has nevertheless been a serious claim that he was also taught by John Bromley. There are two references for Pope's presumed attendance at Bromley's school. The earlier is a letter published by Edmund Curll in 1735 from a correspondent named "E.P.":

> The last school he was put to, before the twelfth year of his age, was in Devonshire Street, near Bloomsbury; there I also was, and the late Duke of Norfolk, at the same time. It was kept by one Bromley, a Popish renegado, who had been a parson, and was one of King James' converts in Oxford,

16. See Note 13 above.
17. Spence, I. 8. Pope *June 1739*, Item 14.
18. Joseph Gillow, *Biographical Dictionary of the English Catholics, from the Breach with Rome in 1534, to the Present Time* (London, 1885-1888, IV. 459.)

George Sherburn (p. 40. n. 2.) in *The Early Career* suggests Father Philips as a possibility for the 'fourth priest.' Pope wrote to Thomas Dancastle on February 18, 1716 concerning Philips ("May your Pouch come swagging home, laden with woodcocks, and may those woodcocks be so fatt & good as to please Mr. Philips.") and to John Dancastle on May 30, 1717 about him ("I encountered Father Philips the other day, on the high way of Salvation of Souls, and I believe suspended a Confession, or reprived a Penance, during the time we drank a Dish of Coffee.") Fr. Philips was the Dancastle's chaplain at the time Pope wrote these letters.

some years after that prince's abdication. He kept a little seminary till, upon an advantageous offer made him, he went a travelling tutor to the present Lord Gage. Mr. Alexander Pope, before he had been four months at this school, or was able to construe Tully's Offices, employed his Muse in satirising his master. It was a libel of at least one hundred verses, which a fellow student having given information of, was found in his pocket, and the young satirist was soundly whipped, and kept prisoner to his room for seven days; whereupon his father fetched him away, and I have been told he never went to school more. How much past correction has wrought upon him, the world is judge; and how much present correction might, may be collected from this sample. I thought it a curious fact, and therefore it is at your service, as one of the ornaments of this excellent person's life. Yours, &c., E.P.[19]

There is little reason to believe that the second source (Charles Dodd's *Church History of England . . . Chiefly With Regard to Catholics*) is independent of Curll.

Although all of the chronological problems regarding Pope's education cannot be satisfied, the following table is perhaps as correct a one as can be compiled in the light of available documentation:

1695-1696: Pope began Latin and Greek under a priest named Banister (perhaps Edward Taverner alias Bannester) also read Ogilvy's Homer and Sandys' Ovid with him;

1696-1697: Pope studied with Edward Taverner at Twyford School;

19. James M. Osborn in a lengthy note (II. 610-611) which serves as an appendix to Item 18 (1. 10) in his Spence edition throws a great deal of light on this difficult matter. "Information about Pope's supposed attendance at a school kept by John Bromley comes from two sources. The second possibly derived from the first. The earlier is a letter published by Curll in 1735 from a correspondent named 'E.P.' . . . The second source is . . . Dodd . . . who wrote that Bromley 'was well skilled in the classicks; and, as I am informed, Mr. *Pope*, the celebrated poet, was one of his pupils.' "

". . . George Sherburn considers that Pope may have written the 'E.P.' letter himself in a deliberate attempt to mislead Curll into inserting mistaken details into his publications."

1697-1700: Pope studied at Thomas Deane's two schools, first at Marylebone and then at Hyde Park Corner;

1700: Pope left Deane's and studied for a few months with a priest at Binfield.

This chronology takes Pope at his word and presumes that the poet's recollections must have precedence over other contemporary documents. If Pope's testimony is given first consideration, he is the most reliable and straightforward guide to his education.

It now remains to be seen what type of teachers and Roman Catholics these various educators were. No additional information can be given on the "fourth priest." There is, however, further documentation available on Edward Taverner and Thomas Deane. Since Pope presumably knew of John Bromley, he will also be discussed.

EDWARD TAVERNER (ALIAS JOHN BANISTER, ALIAS JOHN DAVIS) AND THE TWYFORD SCHOOL

Only a handful of facts are known about Pope's master at Twyford. The first reference to Taverner which can be located is an entry of October, 1685, in the account books of the English College at Madrid (St. George's) where it is stated that "1,000 reales are paid to Fr. Fernando Narbarrete, Rector of St. Alban's, Valladolid, for the keep of the two students, Mr. John Davis and Mr. John Lucas, who arrived on the 25th September to begin their study of philosophy with others who came for St. Alban's College. The two students named are kept at the expense of St. George's."[20] The records of the English College of Valladolid confirm Taverner's entrance date.[21] He said his first Mass at the College at Valladolid on February 22, 1690.[22] Ac-

---

20. *The English College at Madrid, 1611-1767, Publications of the Catholic Record Society, Volume 29,* ed. Canon Edwin Henson (London, 1929), pp. 159-160.

21. *The English College at Valladolid, 1589-1862, Publications of the Catholic Record Society, Volume 30,* ed. Canon Edwin Henson (London, 1930), p. 175n.

22. Canon Henson cites *Liv. 7 Recibos* at Valladolid as his source for the date (*CRS, Volume 30,* p. 176).

cording to the *Libro de Viaticos* at Valladolid, John Lucas, William Calvert and Edward Taverner (written "Taberer" in the entry and signed "Tauerner") left the College on March 26, 1692. Taverner went straight to the Catholic school at Silksteed, near Winchester.[23]

In 1692 the Reverend William Husband, alias Bernard, succeeded the Reverend Thomas Brown, alias Weatherby, as headmaster at Twyford.[24] When Taverner arrived at Silksteed, he assisted Brown in the running of the school. In 1696, Taverner became headmaster, a position he held until 1726.[25] After his retirement, Taverner went to Warkworth Castle where he died in 1745.

If the career of Edward Taverner is sketchy at best, so is the history of Twyford school. The traditional account of Twyford states that at the death of William Husband in 1696 the school, under Taverner's headmastership, moved from Silksteed to Twyford.[26] However, a document in the Lambeth Palace Library suggests a different course of events.

> Within two miles of this place (Silksteed) there is another school, settled in ye midst of a country village called Twyford, wch is flld only with younger children and proves a Nursery to Silksted. . . .[27]

Twyford, established by the same people who had founded Silksteed sometime before 1660, was a school preparatory to Silksteed.

A directive from the Privy Council dated March 7, 1695/6 orders

> that the Schoolmaster and other men and Boyes of the

23. Canon Henson (*CRS, Volume 30*, p. 176) cites the *Libro de Viaticos* as his source for this piece of information. Benson continues: "He [Taverner] went straight to the Catholic school at Silksteed, near Winchester, which about 1696 migrated to Twyford, some two miles away."

24. Bernard Ward, p. 7 gives the following account of the transformation of Twyford School into St. Edmund's College (pp. 3-4).

25. Ward, p. 8.

26. Ward, p. 7 and Wickham, p. 6.

27. Lambeth Palace Library Ms. 993, f. 1696. I am using the citation from the manuscript given by A.C.F. Beales, *Education under Penalty, English Catholic Education from the Reformation to the Fall of James II, 1547-1689* (London, 1963), p. 220.

Popish School at Silksteed near the city of Winchester (be) seized and committed to the Country Gaol in order to be prosecuted according to law, but that the Boyes be discharged and permitted to go to their respective homes.[28]

There is evidence, however, that the school did not disappear or merge into Twyford. At the end of the century, William III was informed "that a Popish school is kept at Silsted near Winchester."[29] Sir John St. Barbe was accordingly instructed to "enquire upon oath as to the persons who keep the school, whether they are legally qualified for it. Ye will send up the information, which are to be handed to the Attorney-General to prosecute the offenders."[30] When St. Barbe sent the affidavits, he was reminded that he did not indicate "whether the school be discontinued, which I desire to know."[31] It obviously had not been suppressed for in February, 1700, the Mayor of Winchester was ordered to "inquire and suppress it."[32] The trouble with the Privy Council in 1695/6 very likely disrupted the Silksteed school seriously enough to merit the transference of some of the Silksteed boys to Twyford. Pope entered Twyford school in the midst of all these difficulties. There is little reason to suspect that he was one of the boys who took part in the migration from Silksteed to Twyford; he was probably not old enough in 1696 to enter Silksteed itself.

It would seem that it was the poet's own satiric attitude toward Taverner which was the decisive factor in his moving from Winchester to London. In any event, by the time Silksteed was running normally again, which was the beginning of 1699 at the earliest, Pope had gone on to Thomas Deane. The Silksteed-Twyford system produced many distinguished graduates in addition to Pope. The Bishops Talbot, their brother the Earl of Shrewsbury, the Earl of Fingal, and many others of the Catholic nobility attended the school.[33] Nathaniel Hooke (d. 1763), the historian and friend of Pope, probably attended the school at the

28. Public Records Office, London. Privy Council Register, 2/76, ff. 317, 354. Quoted by Beales, p. 221.
29. Beales, p. 221. The source for the quotation is not given.
30. *Calendar of State Papers Domestic, 1699-1700*, 294.
31. *Calendar of State Papers Domestic, 1699-1700*, 299.
32. *Calendar of State Papers Domestic, 1699-1700*, 372.
33. Bishop James Talbot (1726-1790), brother of Bishop Thomas Joseph Talbot, is perhaps the most illustrious member of the Catholic clergy to have

same time as the poet. Hooke, also a close friend of Martha Blount, is well known to students of Pope as the Catholic who induced him to confess to a priest on his death-bed.

THOMAS DEANE (1651-1735) OF MARYLEBONE AND HYDE PARK CORNER

Thomas Deane was the son of Edward Deane of Malden, Kent, and was born there in 1651. He entered University College, Oxford, on October 19, 1669. He subscribed to the Articles and took the Oath of Supremacy in the following month when he was probably admitted a servitor. He received his Bachelor's degree in 1673 and the degree of Master of Arts in 1676. He became a tutor in Greek in his college and was elected a fellow of the college on December 4, 1684.

Anthony à Wood in his *Athenae Oxoniensis* says that Deane "declared himself a papist much about the same time that his master, Obadiah Walker, did in March, 1685, whose creature and convert he was."[34] After the landing of the Prince of Orange in England, Deane and John Massey, dean of Christ Church, withdrew from Oxford and went to London. Deane, whose fellowship was declared vacant on February 4, 1688/9, was twice committed to prison in London on the suspicion of being a Jesuit or a priest. On December 18, 1691, he stood in the pillory at Charing Cross under the name of Thomas Franks. He was accused on that occasion of having concealed a libel or pamphlet against the government which had been written by a person living in the same house as he.

There is a gap of nearly five years in Deane's biography from 1691 through 1696. By 1696, however, he was running a school at Marylebone to which Pope was sent. At some time during Pope's stay with him from 1697 through 1700, Deane was forced to move his school to Hyde Park Corner. Weaver Bickerton, an early biographer of Pope, has given an account of the circumstances of the move.

. . . Mr. *Dean* set up the abovementioned Seminary, in

attended Silksteed-Twyford. See J. Kirk, *Biographies of English Catholics in the Eighteenth Century* (1909), p. 228.

34. *Athenae Oxoniensis*, ed. Philip Bliss (London, 1813), IV. 450.

order to procure himself a tolerable Subsistence; but a busy Justice in that neighbourhood [Marylebone], such as the World always has been, and ever will be pester'd with, not contented with the loss he had already sustained, in being deprived of his Fellowship, nor yet with the laborious and disagreeable course of Life, he was obliged to have recourse to for a Livelyhood, being willing to curry Favour with the government, gave him continual Uneasiness; so that he was forced to remove from thence to a House near *Hyde-Park Corner*, on the very spot where *Down-Street* was afterwards built, which having till then belonged to a Nursery-Garden, and consequently having a large open Space adjoining thereto, was not only pleasant and healthy, but perfectly convenient, and the fittest imaginable for the Use for which he designed it.[35]

Neither Bickerton nor any other writer provides many glimpses into the daily workings of either of Deane's schools. Bickerton remarks, however, that

at the Hours of Recreation, whilst the Rest of his School-fellows were diverting themselves at such Games and Sports, as was usual with Boys of their Age, Mr. *Pope* used to amuse himself with Drawing, and such like improving and rational Accomplishments. . . .[36]

The only other piece of biographical material from Deane's teaching days is a letter written to a certain Mr. Pope, the father of a boy at his school in Marylebone:

Honoured Sir,
Your keeping your son so long at home occasions my giving you this trouble to know I have yet mett with no disturbance for these Times, nor am apprehensive of any as being no military man. Many surprising things have happened of late, but God will bring to light the Truth of Kings & the wickedness & Cursedness of Men. A line or two from your self of your Resolutions concerning the disposing of the child & also of your own welfare would be a great

35. Weaver Bickerton, *Life of Alexander Pope* (London, 1744), pp. 12-13.
36. Bickerton, pp. 13-14. Spence believed that the play based on the *Iliad* which Pope composed for his schoolfellows was composed by Pope while he was at Deane's (Spence's index to the Huntington manuscript).

satisfaction to me that I am [*sic*] may not know you have not forgotten

	Honoured Sir
Marti 27, 1696	Your most obliged humble servant
	Tho: Deane

Sir my very humble service to your Lady & kind remembrance to the Child.[37]

Pope himself has left some indication in his correspondence with John Caryll (one of whose sons also attended Deane's school) of his attitude towards his former schoolmaster. In 1727, when the following sentiments were expressed, Deane was in prison for a "seditious pamphlet" and Pope, who had spoken unfavourably of Deane in the past, was contributing to a pension for him.

> The subject of the letter which miscarried, was Mr. Dean, my old master, who had writ me one whereby I perceived his head happy in the highest self opinion, whatever became of his body. And hereupon writ you a dissertation proving it better for him to remain a prisoner than to have his liberty. I showed, that self-conceit is the same with respect to the philosopher, as a good conscience to a religious man, a perpetual feast, &c. But to be serious, I've told Mr. Webb that I will contribute with Lord Dormer and you in what manner you shall agree to think most effectual for his relief. My own judgment indeed is, that giving him a small yearly pension among us and others, even where he is, would keep him out of harms-way: which writing and publishing of books may bring him into. And that I find to be the project that bites him. He was all his life a dupe to some project or other.[38]

The *General Evening Post* for November 15, 1735, contains the news of Deane's death "a few Days ago. . .in the 108th Year of his Age, at Mrs. Wagstaff's in Suffolk Place, near St. George's Fields, Southwark." The obituary notes that he lived in later life "wholly upon charitable Contributions."

---

37. This letter in the Lambeth Palace Library is transcribed in *Miscellanea*, Volume LVI of the Publication of the Catholic Record Society, ed. E. T. Reynolds (Newport, 1964) in Section II, "Papers from the Lambeth Palace Library," ed. Carson I. A. Ritchie, p. 113.

38. *The Correspondence of Alexander Pope*, ed. George Sherburn (Oxford, 1956), II. 428. The letter to Caryll is dated March 28 and is assigned by

Both Wood and Pope looked upon Deane as a "dupe" or "creature" of others. It is difficult to accept such a conjecture on Deane's character in toto, but it is true that Deane's life was very much influenced by Obadiah Walker. Walker (1616-1699) is one of the most celebrated English converts to Roman Catholicism in the seventeenth century. A fellow, and later master, of University College, Oxford, Walker's life was one long flirtation with Catholicism. Some time after July, 1648, Walker journeyed to Rome "improving himself in all kinds of polite literature."[39] Upon his return to England, he became the tutor to a son of a Mr. Hildyard and supposedly converted the boy to Catholicism. In 1676, Walker became master of University College. Dealings which Walker had with Abraham Woodhead's "popish seminary" at Hoxton caused his conduct to be noted in the House of Commons towards the end of November, 1678. He was "much suspected at this time to be a papist" and, "had not Mr. Walker had a friend in the house who stood up for him, he would have had a messenger sent for him." However, early in the following year, Walker emphatically denied being a Papist. In April, 1679, Sir Harbottle Grimson mentioned Walker's name in a speech calling the attention of the House of Commons to the printing of popish books at the theatre at Oxford. A complaint was made to the vice-chancellor in June, 1680, of a sermon preached by one of Walker's pupils at St. Mary's, and the booksellers in Oxford were forbidden to sell his book, *The Benefits of our Saviour Jesus Christ to Mankind*, because it smacked of Catholicism.

Upon the accession of James II to the throne, Walker's sympathetic attitude towards Catholicism became very clear-cut, and, through his friendship with James, Walker received a great many privileges. In April, 1686, Mass was held in Walker's lodgings, and in the following month the Master and three others were granted a royal license and dispensation "to absent themselves from the church, common prayer, and from taking oaths of supremacy and allegiance." In the same month, Walker

Sherburn to the year 1727. Sherburn comments on this letter in note 2 on pp. 39-40 of *The Early Career*: "One may guess from this letter that Pope is writing to the fathers of his fellow students under Deane. Among these would be, then, John Caryll, Jr., Webb (who married the widow of Pope's friend Henry Englefield), and Charles Dormer, who being a Catholic priest did not assume the title of Baron Dormer when his father died in 1728."

39. Smith, *Annals of University College* [as quoted in *DNB*].

was also granted permission to print for twenty-one years a list of thirty-seven Catholic works (the only restriction being that the sale in any one year was not to exceed twenty thousand). A private press for the printing of these books was erected in University College in the following year.

The arrival of the printing press at Walker's lodgings brings Thomas Deane back into the picture. During the course of the events just described, Deane was a fervent disciple of Walker's and, as Wood says, was converted to Catholicism through him. The best evidence for Deane's participation in Walker's activities is the publication in 1688 of Deane's *The Religion of Mar. Luther Neither Catholick nor Protestant, Prov'd from his own Works.* The title page of *The Religion* states that it was printed by "Henry Cruttenden, One of his Majesty's Printers. MDCLXXXVIII." However, a manuscript note (in seventeenth-century script) in the British Library's copy states, "This is one of the privately printed books in Obadiah Walker's Lodgings in University College."[40] The tract is in two parts: Part One is divided into two sections, I. *LUTHER's Religion not Catholick, in Eight Instances.* and II. *LUTHER's Religion not Protestant, in Eight Instances;* Part Two, *REFLECTIONS in Answer to the Vindication of Martin Luther's Spirit, Printed at the Theater in Oxford* is a defense of Abraham Woodhead's *Discourse concerning the Spirit of Luther* against an attack made upon it by Francis Atterbury, later Bishop of Rochester in *An Answer to some Considerations in the Spirit of Martin Luther* (1687).[41]

The Religion is typical of the Roman Catholic apologia of

40. The following information, in a different hand from that giving the details on the printing of the book, is found in the space facing the title page: "Register of Convocation Bb. 318. Whereas William Gilbert of Oriel Coll: was entered in University Coll: in Mich: terme on the 16th day of December, 1687, and is of full standing for his degree of Bachelor of Arts from his admission; but being not Matriculated in due time by the fault of Mr. Obadiah Walker the then Master, who on the last day of the Terme when he espected [sic] to be Matriculated, told him he should not tarry in his College, unlesse he would take Mr. Deane, a known Papist, to be his Tutor, and be as he termed it, of the true, that is the Romish Religion, which he absolutely refusing, lost the benefit of the Terme. . . ."

41. Pope was, of course, a close friend of Atterbury's and corresponded with him on literary matters (Atterbury was an advocate of blank verse). The most famous incident in their friendship is Pope's testifying on May 8, 1723 at Atterbury's trial before the House of Lords for treason. The object of Pope's testimony was to demonstrate that during his visits at the Deanery and At-

its time. Like many Catholic controversialists, Deane puts great stress on the Real Presence.

> Concerning the *Administration of the Word and Sacraments*, Luther teaches, *that all men (and women also) have authority and power to administer.* These are his own words, *The first Office of a Priest is to preach the Word,* &c. . . .Nay, *Luther* proceeded so far herein, that (as Dr. Covel witnesses, in his Defence of Mr. *Hooker, art.* 15. *p.* 101) he was not afraid to affirm, *that the Sacraments were effectual, tho administred by Satan himself.*[42]

> To the Proof of *Luther's* setting up his own Authority against the Church, and maintaining his own Doctrines as infallible, nothing is answer'd. The instance which the *Considerer* gives, is the Doctrine of *Consubstantiation* wherein *Luther* pretends Certainty and Revelation in God's Word. Could any man *have persuaded me* (says *Luther's Epist. ad Argent.*) there was nothing but *Bread and Wine in the Sacrament, he had much oblig'd me. For being in great perplexity, I took great pains in Discussing the point; I endeavour'd with all my might to extricate and free my self, as well perceiving I should thereby very much incommode the Papcy. But I see I am caught, there is no way of escaping left me: For the words of the Evangelist This is my Body, &c.) are too plain and clear to be forc'd to any other meaning.* It is evident, that in this Doctrine *Luther* was neither *Catholick,* nor Church of *England Protestant.* But yet so much a *Catholick* he was, as to hold the *real presence of the Body and Blood of our Lord in the Sacrament.*[43]

To Deane has been attributed *An Essay towards a Proposal for Catholick Communion* (1705), but the real author was probably Joshua Bassett.[44] The other tracts by Deane cannot be identified.

---

terbury's seat at Bromley the Bishop had never shown any evidence that he was taking part in a conspiracy. On the contrary, Pope had heard him express sentiments of loyalty. *Early Career*, pp. 223-230, has detailed information on this matter. See also Maynard Mack, "Letters of Pope to Atterbury in the Tower," *R.E.S.*, Vol. 21 (1945), 117-125.

42. Thomas Deane, *The Religion of Mar. Luther Neither Catholick nor Protestant, Prov'd from his own Works* (Oxford, 1688), pp. 4-5.

43. Deane, p. 13. See chapters 5 and 6 for Pope's interest in the doctrine of "the word becoming flesh" in *The Rape of the Lock* and *The Dunciads*.

44. See Gillow (I. 152) for information on Bassett.

In any event, the man with whom Pope studied for approximately three years had been at the forefront in the Walker
controversy at Oxford during the reign of James II and was
engaged throughout most of his adult life in Catholic polemics.

JOHN BROMLEY (d. 1717) OF BLOOMSBURY

Although there is only the slightest possibility that Pope
actually studied with John Bromley, there is definite and acceptable evidence, as has been shown, to indicate that Pope knew
that Bromley's school, extensively patronized by the better-class
Catholics, existed at the time he would have been able to attend
it.[45]

Bromley, a native of Shropshire, received an academical
education. He may be the John Bromley of Christ Church,
Oxford, who received the degrees of Bachelor of Arts in 1685 and
Master of Arts in 1688. In the beginning of James II's reign, he
was a curate at St. Giles'-in-the-Fields, London. Soon afterwards,
Bromley joined the Roman Catholic Church and obtained
employment as a corrector in the king's printing house. On being
deprived of his position there, Bromley established a boarding-
school in London. "He was skilled in the classicks" and was
allowed to teach in Bloomsbury by a dispensation from James II
issued in February, 1687.[46] After the dissolution of the school, he
was appointed tutor to some young gentlemen. Like Deane,
Bromley was also a Roman Catholic apologist. His writings,
however, consist in translations and not original pieces of
controversial literature. He published his translation of *The
Catechism for the Curats, Compos'd by the Decree of the Council
of Trent, and Publish'd by Command of Pope Pius the Fifth* in
1687. He may also be the translator of *The Canons and Decrees
of the Council of Trent* published in the same year.

There is some evidence to suggest that the course of
Bromley's conversion may have taken place under conditions
similar to those of Thomas Deane's. While he was in his second
year at Christ Church, Obadiah Walker's friend, John Massey, is
said to have been appointed dean of Christ Church. This may

45. See note 19 above.
46. Beales, p. 237.

have been the beginning of Bromley's inclination towards Catholicism. Also, Henry Hills, the printer of Bromley's translations, was licensed to print books at about the same time as Obadiah Walker, the only other Catholic ever licensed by James to print.[47] Bromley, then, was in the same Roman Catholic controversialist circles as Walker and Deane.

"All the teaching I had,. . .God knows,. . .extended a very little way."

The system of education to which Pope was subjected as a young boy was never meant to do for Roman Catholics what the public schools were doing for their Protestant peers.[48] Also the elementary system devised by Catholics in England was not intended in any way to duplicate the system established in Flanders and France by Catholics in England. Catholics of this period looked to the continent for their education. The purpose of the schools in Britain at this time was to prepare both boys and girls for the colleges and convent-schools abroad. The school systems of Douay, St. Omers, and elsewhere required that youngsters on coming to them should be able to read and write and have been instructed in the rudiments of Latin.[49] The

47. Beales, p. 237.

48. I am indebted to William F. Hastings' unpublished 1923 M.A. thesis (University of London), "The Education of English Catholics, 1559-1800" (especially pp. 342, 359-360, 384-385, and 388) for the general remarks above and have paraphrased freely from the pages indicated. I have also profited from A.C.F. Beales' study (cited above) and from W.A.L. Vincent's *The Grammar Schools, Their Continuing Tradition, 1660-1714* (London, 1969). John Bossy's *The English Catholic Community* (New York, 1976) should also be consulted.

It is difficult to be very precise about the differences between Pope's education and that of the Anglican and nonconformist boy. It must be remembered that the type of training Pope received was entirely preparatory to the more advanced and sophisticated curriculum available on the Continent (Pope evidently did not think very much of the standards there: ". . . for it seems at St. Omer's they do not learn English grammar," Pope to Caryll, July 19, 1711, *Correspondence*, I. 127). The Anglican system was continuous whereas the Catholic, which shared many of the same basic aims, was sharply divided into two parts. The Catholic system undoubtedly suffered from this disjunction. The nonconformist schools emphasized training in modern languages (a trait shared by the Catholics whose children often continued their education abroad) and science. See Foster Watson, *The English Grammar Schools to 1660* (Cambridge, 1908), pp. 534-536 for a discussion of the different aims of the Anglican and nonconformist systems.

49. Hastings cites *Rules and Regulations of St. Omers 1600* and *Ratio Studiorum, Reg. Praef. Studior. Inf.* as the sources for this regulation.

schools that Pope went to, then, were meant to be preparatory schools for the institutions for English Catholics established on the continent.

A second point has to be made before describing the type of education Pope received. Pope's education follows trends in Catholic education from 1688 onwards. The religious orders, especially the Jesuits, had been the dominant force in English Catholic education before the Revolution. The history of Pope's education, however, parallels the increase in the number of schools kept by lay-schoolmasters and by secular priests.

Before 1688, the secular clergy, who should have been the dominant missionary force, were sufficiently large in number, but their actual condition was wholly unsatisfactory. Activities and movements were largely undirected. Further, they were disturbed and disrupted by domestic controversy. Episcopal succession was probably the most important problem. Added to this were the arch-priest debate, pro-Jesuit and anti-Jesuit feelings, the different outlook in the older (or seminary) clergy as to methods of procedure. These factors tended to demoralise the seculars and render them inefficient. In contrast, the members of the Society of Jesus acted as a compact body of Catholic clergymen. One of the most significant religious-educational features of James II's reign was the re-organization of the secular clergy. At the king's command, four districts or vicariates, each governed by a vicar-apostolic, were established.

This arrangement had a definite educational import. The revolution of 1688 brought complete ruin to the Jesuits, and the seculars were ready to take over their work. (The Silksteed-Twyford-Longwood schools and that of the Franciscans at Amestherley were the only Catholic institutions of any importance to survive 1688.)

The events of 1688 acted as a catalyst for a strong Catholic secular priesthood to replace the religious communities, and the course of Pope's education reproduces chronologically this historical evolution. He was at school under a secular priest, Father Taverner, for a year; he then studied with a prominent layman, Thomas Deane.

If the course of the Catholic education Pope received can be placed in a convenient historical framework, the actual matter of that education cannot. The general organization of the schools he attended can be gathered from existing documents, but the actual curriculum is a completely different matter. In order to gain as precise an idea as possible of that education, it might be best to examine it under three headings: the general organization of a Catholic school 1660-1750; the teaching of languages in those schools; and finally the matter of moral or ethical training.

Organization. Luckily, the 1743 "Terms of Admission" for Twyford have survived,[50] and these will give a clear picture of the type of environment Pope found himself in at eight years of age when he went there.

The entering student had the choice of bringing with him two pairs of sheets, six napkins, a knife, fork, and spoon or paying two pounds in lieu of these. The parents of each child paid eighteen pounds per annum for board and tuition at the school (the prospectus mentions English, Latin, and Greek as the subjects of tuition; French was optional at two pounds extra). One had to pay extra for lessons in "writing and ciphering" (three pounds) and in dancing (also three pounds). There was one lesson in Geography (10/6) which was "taken out of Thursday, their weekly payday." The boarders were not allowed their own pocket money, "but whatever their Parents think fit to allow them per week is given them once a fortnight and charged quarterly. None have more than 6d. or less than 3d. per Week." The boys were "allowed Flesh meat only once a day, viz.: at dinner, but then they are not stinted but may send for it as often as they please & never sit down to less than two sorts of meat on meat days, generally boiled and roast." The students always rose between six and seven in the morning and went to bed between eight and nine.

> They play under ye eye of their Masters in Recreation time;
> for which end, as well as to promote their health (to which

50. The "Terms of Admission" for Twyford are quoted in full in "College Notes," *The Ushaw Magazine,* XIV (March, July, December 1909), 111-114. The "Terms" are dated 1743. It seems doubtful that the daily regime at the school would have been much different in Pope's time. *The Rules of the Schools at the Jesuits in Fenchurch-Street* (1688) are similar to the 1743 "Terms." Rogers (cited above) quotes from the rules and customs of Standon School, the successor to the Twyford school. The children there experienced a regime similar to the one at Twyford and read such classics as were suitable "to their Age & Capacity, as 1st the Doway Abstract, with Mr. Gother's Instructions for Children, 2ndly, Fleury's Historical Catechism, 3rdly, Tuberville's &c., with the Chief Master's Approbation. The short Abridgement of the Christian Doctrine is indeed the Catechism in use for Children very young" (239).

exercise is so conducive) a spacious & commodious place for playing at Fives or handball has been lately finished, consisting of a high wall yt joins to ye House & is carried on above 70ft. in length and of a brick pavement of ye same length & 36ft. in breadth.[51]

The boys were allowed to go for walks on Sundays, holidays, and, weather permitting, for a fixed period each day. These walks were always in the company of a master who prevented "their having any communication with ye Parish children, which is strictly forbid. . .by which means & precautions 'tis hoped they will be kept strangers to Vice and Immorality." The Vacation times were a week at Easter, a fortnight at Christmas, and a month following Corpus Christi.

Instruction in languages was certainly the most important part of the curriculum of any school — Catholic or Protestant — of the period. It is almost impossible to discover by what methods the students at Twyford and Marylebone/Hyde Park Corner were taught Latin and Greek. Pope told Spence that under Father Bannester, he learned "accidence and the Greek elements."[52] "He began for Latin and Greek together (which is the way in the schools of the Jesuits, and which he seemed to think a good way)."[53] Pope also told Spence that "with the two latter masters [I] lost what little I had got under my first."[54] It is difficult to know how Pope may have been "untaught." Perhaps the most intelligent suggestion is that Taverner and Deane may have been employing in grammar the methods of two Roman Catholic authors who seem to have experienced a vogue well into the eighteenth century, William Bathe (Bateus) and Dr. Joseph Webbe.

William Bathe (1564-1614) was born at Dublin on Easter Sunday, 1564, the son of John Bathe, a judge, and his wife,

51. "Terms," on p. 113 of *Ushaw Magazine.*

52. Spence, I. 10. Pope *18-21 January 1743*, Item 18.

53. Spence, I. 9. Pope 1742, Item 15. Latin and Greek were certainly not begun together at other schools in England of the same period. However, *The Rules of the Schools . . . in Fenchurch Street* does state under rule two: "These schools are common to all, of what condition, soever, and none shall be excluded when they shall be thought fit to begin to learn Latin, and Write sufficiently well: And in these Schools shall be taught Greek and Latin, as also Poetry and Rhetoric, as they shall rise to higher Schools."

54. Spence, 8. Pope *June 1739*, Item 14.

Eleanor Preston. He was brought up a Protestant, but, while under the care of a Catholic tutor, he became a Catholic. Wood says that he studied for several years at Oxford, but he does not indicate what college or hall he attended or whether he took a degree. After Oxford, "under pretence of being weary with the heresy professed in England,"[55] Bathe went to the continent where he became a member of the Society of Jesus. He studied at Louvain and Padua. He was later appointed rector of the Irish College at Salamanca. Bathe died at Madrid on June 17, 1614.

Of Bathe's six major works, three deal with Christian doctrine, one with music, and two with Latin. The *Ianua Linguarum* (1611) is the more famous of the two Latin treatises. Comenius wrote at a later time of his own subsequently published *Janua* that

> it was published with a slight change of title. For I had been advised by someone that there was already extant such a book, containing the whole of the Latin language, called *Ianua Linguarum,* the work of Irish monks; but when I had seen it, I perceived it to be written without orderly arrangement of the materials.[56]

Bathe's work, however, was intended primarily as a guide for the Catholic missionaries in the New World, in learning the native languages and in teaching the Indians Latin. Comenius is certainly right in disclaiming Bathe as a source: Bathe's book, despite some superficial similarities, is not based on Comenius' conception of a natural ordering of words. However, it is difficult to determine the printing history of Bathe's work in English because it has often been confused with Comenius' book. The best estimate is that Bathe's *Ianua* went through nine editions (about 11,000 copies) after its first printing in English in 1615. "The Puritan associates of Comenius in his 'scholastic endeavours' knew it [Bathe's book] well."[57]

The basis of Bathe's system is a series of sentences (1200 in

55. *DNB*, III. 402-403. All the biographical material on Bathe in the text is taken from *DNB*.

56. Beale (p. 196) quotes from the 1633 *Janua* of Comenius.

57. Timothy Corcoran, *Studies in the History of Classical Teaching* (Dublin and Belfast, 1911), p. 105. Corcoran is the source for the information given on the printing history of Bathe's *Ianua* in English. Despite the title, Corcoran's book is concerned almost exclusively with Bathe.

all) divided into Centuries. The student commits these sentences to memory as the first step in learning Latin. "The Centuries" are grouped into meaningful sequential patterns (e.g., *Centuria secunda* concerns prudence and imprudence, and *Centuria quinque* contains a sequence on the Passion of Christ).[58] The student is thus instructed in moral virtue as he proceeds through the fundamentals of Latin.

Joseph Webbe (fl. 1612-1626) was English and Roman Catholic by birth. He graduated M.D. and Ph.D. from a continental university, perhaps Padua. In 1612 he published at Rome an astrological work entitled *Minae Coelestus affectus aegrotantibus denunciates hoc anno 1612.* Sometime before 1622, Webbe returned to England and in 1623 was residing in the Old Bailey. Webbe strongly advocated a colloquial method of teaching languages, proposing to extend it even to the classical tongues, and to substitute it for the pedantic manner of grammatical study then in general use. In 1622, he published *An Appeale to Truth, in the Controuersie betweene Art and Vse,* which he supplemented with *A Petition to the High Court of Parliament, in behalf of auncient and authentique Authors.* In the latter work, Webbe claims that his system received encouragement from James I and that he wishes to have the sole right to teach by this method.[59]

It is, of course, impossible to speculate with much confidence on the type of language training Pope received. Pope's comment that he "lost what little" he had achieved under his first master may simply mean that Taverner and Deane were poor teachers. However, Pope may have been expressing his impatience with the avant-garde language teaching devised by two prominent Catholic pedagogues.

Moral Indoctrination. Although one has to speculate also on the nature of the moral training given at Pope's schools, the

---

58. The "Hymnus de Passione Christi" on page 30 of the 1615 London edition faces "A Hymne vpon the Passion of Christ" on page 31. The first three sentences in each section are:

455 Coenam cum Discipulis celebrauit.
455 Christ celebrated his Supper with his Disciples.
456 Cobitum Apostolis palam nunciauit.
456 He openly told his death to his Apostles.
457 Ac authorem sceleris simul demonstrauit.
457 And withall shewed them the Author of that wicked act.

conjectures have more of an air of certainty about them. The Twyford prospectus contains one hint on the matter.

> At their studies they [the boys] are constantly attended by a proper Master, & have every day except Thursday a lesson set them to learn by heart in some Catechism suitable to their age & capacity, which is carefully expounded to them every Sunday.[60]

There is one work which one may be certain Thomas Deane paid a great deal of attention to: Obadiah Walker's *Of Education, especially of young Gentlemen* (Oxford, 1673; sixth edition by 1699). In his Preface, Walker states how his tract is in a slightly different mould from contemporary treatises on education:

> It is not the design of this Discourse to intrench upon any knowledg already disposed, and appropriated into Arts and Sciences, as they are at this time delivered; but only to propose such things to consideration and use, as, lying scattered and in common, are less cultivated and regarded. For this reason 'tis vain to expect accurateness of method or stile; but the first part is almost wholly writ in manner of *Essaies,* the second of Aphorismes: the stiles most free, loose, and unscientifical.
>
> The most useful knowledg is that, of a mans self: and this depends upon that more universal consideration of *Quid homo potest*; naturally, and artificially: *i.e.* what abilities are in us originally, by the gift of God; and what attainable by our own industry. And both these in order to *Knowledg* or *Action*. . . .
>
> The perfecting of a young man in *Sciences* and *Speculative Learning* is the business of so many Books and Persons; that it seems superfluous to engage in that part of Instruction. It was therefore thought more useful to furnish some rules and principles of *Active life*; as being that, whereto Gentlemen seem more disposed by their births, and general inclinations; and whereto also little assistance could be expected from our ordinary speculations. I have therefore rather chused to gather up disorderly, and bind together,

---

59. All biographical material on Webbe is from the *DNB*.
60. *Ushaw Magazine*, 113.

such scattered counsels and notions, as have occured either in observation, or in some *Italian* Writers, not ordinarily amongst us.[61]

Walker's miniature Castiglione for young men contains a philosophy of a speculative nature about the conduct of one's private and personal life. The poet who was to write so magnificently of the ruling passion may have been instructed at a very early age on the diverse "inclinations, and dispositions of Man, and the ways to rectify and order them."[62]

> *Passions are the natural motions of the Soul towards objects agreeable or disagreeable.* Or *the motions, or effects, which objects pleasing or displeasing immediately cause in the Soul.* i.e. what the Soul suffers from its objects immediately without deliberation. Tho some call *Passions* only the more *irregular and ungoverned* actions of the Soul.
>
> *Inclinations are the frequenter, and customary working according to those passions.* And, if meerly according to natural suggestions, they are properly called *Inclinations*: but if they proceed to excess, and be not bridled and regulated, they become *vices*. But if regulated by reason or Gods spirit, they are properly *Virtues*.[63]

Again, speculations are difficult to make on the precise kind of moral education Pope received as a young boy. It seems, however, that his teachers had manuals derived from earlier, or even contemporary, courtesy books which would have allowed them to impart to their charges a basic practical and philosophical sense of what it was to be a Catholic in late seventeenth-century England.[64]

CONCLUSIONS

The detailed presentation of Pope's probable education does

---

61. Obadiah Walker, *Education, Especially of Young Gentlemen* (Oxford, 1673), pp. A3-5.

62. Walker, p. 71.

63. Walker, pp. 71-72.

64. Francis Hawkins' *Youths Behaviour, or Decency in Conversation Amongst Men Composed in French by grave Persons, for the Use and Benefit of their Youth* (6th edition: 1654) was a manual of practical instruction on such diverse subjects as writing letters, combing one's hair, and "Walking with thy Superiour bow."

lead to a re-consideration of some aspects of the poet's early life. None of Pope's contemporary biographers — nor any of the recent lives, even Sherburn's — gives the reader a sense of the awesome difficulties which still attended being a Catholic in the last part of the seventeenth century: this remark is especially true of Pope's education.

Edward Taverner was educated in an English college on the continent. Thomas Deane lost his position at Oxford because of his conversion to Rome and was pilloried at Charing Cross. A "busy justice" forced him to move from Marylebone to Hyde Park Corner. He was in the midst of Obadiah Walker's circle at Oxford and, under Walker's influence, a controversialist writer of some stature. John Bromley, a teacher Pope most certainly knew of, was a translator of Council of Trent documents. All of these events are common enough to the student of recusant history of the period, but the immediacy of such events in the daily life of Alexander Pope as a young person has never been stressed adequately. Pope was educated by men who had suffered at first hand for their profession of the Catholic faith. These teachers were not only Catholics — they were, especially in the case of Thomas Deane, Catholics with a real post-Reformation, post-Trent sense of their religion.

The course of Pope's education also shows the clear historical progression in the development of Catholic education in England from the hands of the Jesuits and other religious orders into those of secular priests and laymen. Still, it is extraordinarily difficult to come to any sort of understanding of how much the curriculum he was trained in influenced the future poet. Bathe's moralistic sentences may have had some influence on Pope's particular use of the aphoristic, terse couplet. And the poet of the "ruling passion" may have found his first inspirations in the moral *dicta* of such writers as Obadiah Walker.

The implications of Pope's Catholic education are suggestive even though it is difficult to be certain of any definite influences on the poetry. However, there can be no doubt that the poet was not born into a Catholicism that simply impeded his ability to live in Westminster or that prevented him from owning land. At the very least, Pope must have learned from his schoolmasters that he was a Catholic born into arduous times.

James King

The Cure of Body and Soul
at the Paris Hospital
at the End of the Old Regime*

One of the commonplaces of modern medicine is that the physician is the undisputed head of the medical team. Under his direction both nurses and elaborate technical and other support personnel of the hospital serve the patient in a unified, coordinated effort.[1] Until relatively recently, this was not at all the case. Professional nursing was not yet born in the eighteenth century.[2] Medical intervention was still woefully wanting in therapeutic success and was often hamstrung by institutional and traditional authority.[3] The modern hospital was in the process of becoming.[4] While the administration of the municipal hospital of Paris, which furnished the central focus of this paper, had for nearly 300 years before the French Revolution been consigned to secular hands,[5] clerical influence remained exceedingly strong there. The hospital nurses to whom the sick poor were entrusted from admission to discharge were regular clergy representing the

* The author wishes to thank the Prioress, Sister St. Roch of the Religieuses Augustines de l'Hôtel-Dieu de Paris, and the Secretary-General, Sister St. Michel, who graciously permitted me to work in the archives of their community; the Abbé Charles Molette and my friend Professor Guillaume de Bertier de Sauvigny for their helpfulness in Paris; and my wife Dr. Hilda B. Greenbaum who prepared the appendices.
1. H. C. Moidel, G. E. Sorenson, E. C. Geblin, and M. A. Kaufmann, *Nursing Care of the Patient with Medical and Surgical Disorders* (New York, 1971), p. 6; M. A. Mason, *Basic Medical-Surgical Nursing* (New York, 1967), p. 9.
2. R. H. Shryock, *The History of Nursing* (Philadelphia, 1959), pp. 217-36; L. R. Seymer, *A General History of Nursing* (London, 1932), pp. 63-66; A. E. Pavey, *The Story of the Growth of Nursing* (London, 1959), pp. 238-43.
3. A. Castiglioni, *A History of Medicine*, E. B. Krumbhaar, trans., (New York, 1958), pp. 650-66; L. S. King, *The Road to Medical Enlightenment, 1650-1695* (London-New York, 1970), pp. 1-14; P. Gay, "The Enlightenment as Medicine and Cure," in *The Age of Enlightenment: Studies Presented to Theodore Besterman* (Edinburgh, 1967), pp. 375-86.
4. J. D. Thompson and G. Goldin, *The Hospital: A Social and Architectural History* (New Haven, 1975), pp. 79-155.
5. For legislation of 1505 and later, see E. Coyecque, *L'Hôtel-Dieu de Paris au moyen âge*, (Paris, 1891), I: 184-99.

ancient and lofty vocation of Christian hospitality within an institution whose very name, Hôtel-Dieu (House of God), bore witness to the dignity of their calling. Their conviction was that the first obligation of healing was to cure the soul and then the body.

The Enlightenment, which forged dynamic and enduring innovations in science, politics, economics, ethics, and social organization, was equally influential in medicine, particularly in the evolution of architectural, organizational, and functional forms of the new hospital within whose walls a rigorous, scientific medicine, "clinical medicine," was being taught.[6] Within the Hôtel-Dieu a group of physicians and surgeons was determined to secure the dominion of medicine and the new medical education which they pioneered within the hospital setting. They held that the competing practices of religious nursing were injurious to health and imperiled the curative mission. The sisters, upholders of a healing tradition which long antedated the arrival of the lay doctor, met the challenge. An acrimonious struggle ensued because they refused to yield up their inspired prerogatives. What follows are the circumstances leading up to this clash.

In the summer of 1787 Parisians exulted in Louis XVI's order to build four new hospitals in the open spaces and fresh air of the suburbs of the capital to replace the overcrowded, hopelessly antiquated Hôtel-Dieu on the city isle.[7] While historians have been attentive to reform projects throughout the century to relocate the universally-condemned municipal hospital,[8] they have not taken cognizance of important internal changes which were initiated by reformers determined that remedying abuses could not wait for new buildings.[9] In July 1787 a comprehensive code of fifty-two articles, regulating the full

6. E. H. Ackerknecht, *Medicine at the Paris Hospital, 1794-1848* (Baltimore, 1967), pp. 3-28.

7. L. S. Greenbaum, "Jean-Sylvain Bailly, the Baron de Breteuil and the 'Four New Hospitals' of Paris," *Clio Medica,* VIII (1973) :1 261-84, which furnishes the basis for a similar discussion in *Les Machines à guérir: aux origines de l'hôpital moderne,* M. Foucault et al. eds., (Paris, 1977), pp. 92-96.

8. These are summarized in M. Candille, "Les projets de translation de l'Hôtel-Dieu de Paris hors de la Cité," *Rev. Assist. Pub. à Paris,* VI (1956): 743-56, VII (1957): 239-63, 343-59, 433-49.

9. An incomplete summary may be read in M. Fosseyeux, *L'Hôtel-Dieu de Paris aux XVIIe et XVIIIe siècles* (Paris, 1912), pp. 342-44.

gamut of medical services and patient care, was put into operation.[10] The code was drawn up by Jean Colombier, distinguished military physician and royal inspector of civil hospitals and prisons,[11] who for eight years before his death in 1789 supervised the reconstruction of the hospital. The code was approved by the trustees of the Hôtel-Dieu on July 16,[12] in time for the reopening of one of the hospital's two wings, burned out in 1772 and rebuilt after 1781 at considerable expense by the government under Colombier's painstaking supervision.[13] The implementation of these regulations fell to the eminent surgeon and teacher, Pierre-Joseph Desault, since 1786 first-surgeon of the Hôtel-Dieu and head of a staff of 107 surgeons. For Desault the code was the gateway to the inauguration within the hospital of a surgery school and clinic which he wished to make the leading educational and therapeutic institution of its kind in the kingdom.

By spirit and intent the new code envisioned the Hôtel-Dieu as a health center for the treatment of acute and chronic disease, organized and governed in accordance with diagnostic and therapeutic requirements. Now, for the first time,[14] the full range of medical intervention — admission, examination,

10. M. Brièle, ed., *Délibérations de l'ancien bureau de l'Hôtel-Dieu,* (Paris, 1883), II: 186-89, 198-99 [Hereafter *"Délibérations HD"*]. The original is in Archives de l'Assistance Publique de Paris [Hereafter "AAPP"], "Registre des délibérations au bureau de l'Hôtel-Dieu de Paris. Année 1787 (Volume 157), fols. 468-74 [Hereafter "Registre HD"].

11. Colombier's authorship is confirmed in a letter of December 3 1787 in Archives Nationales de France [Hereafter "AN"] F[15] 233. On Colombier, see P.-L.-M.-J. Gallot-Lavallée, *Un Hygiéniste au XVIIIe siècle, Jean Colombier* (Paris, 1913).

12. The daily operations of the hospital and the promulgation of regulations, like those of July 1787 were vested in an administration of twelve prominent citizens of Paris, magistrates, financiers, and lawyers of the various tribunals of Paris who enjoyed life tenure. Their policies and legislation were ratified at regular meetings by a board of governors, seven trustees who exercised legal authority for the hospital, dignitaries of church (Archbishop of Paris), crown (Lieutenant-General of Police), magistracy (First-President of the Paris parlement, Attorney-General of the same body, First-President of the *Cour des aides,* First President of the *Chambre des comptes*) and the City of Paris (Provost of Merchants).

13. The record of his close collaboration with the architect and Superintendent of Buildings of the Hôtel-Dieu, Bonnot, on every detail connected with the reconstruction may be read in *Délibérations HD*, pp. 92-252.

14. Ibid, p. 219.

diagnosis, feeding, treatment and discharge — were to be subject to rigorous regulation and faithful recording in patient case-records. These procedures were defined as clinical functions and were vested in the hands of staff physicians and surgeons under whose direction the nurses of the hospital were to serve.

To the sixty-nine mostly elderly Augustinian nurses of the Hôtel-Dieu,[15] who commanded a domestic staff of 400 to help care for 2500-3000 patients,[16] this kind of hospital was not at all acceptable. For 1200 years, they argued, the Hôtel-Dieu had been a "hospice of religion,"[17] a house which belonged to them and to the poor, a shelter of charity and consolation which accepted all men, sick or hungry, in accord with the Christian ideal of hospitality. And for all that time, the nuns claimed, they had been sovereign custodians of the sick, "without intermediary." Their authority was superior to physicians and surgeons whom they considered "strangers" who sold their services and who, lacking holy vows, could not be genuinely committed to the welfare of the sick.[18] The sisters reviled the purely therapeutic hospital of the eighteenth century which cared for physical maladies alone.[19] They distrusted new policy departures of the

15. The median age of the sisters was fifty-three. See Appendix I.

16. The nuns were assisted by ten novices, twenty "girls of the upper chamber" who worked without vows or pay, 162 male and 146 female orderlies and nurses in wards and service rooms, thirty-eight laundry domestics and twenty supernumerary servants (AAPP, Liasse 80. "Etat général des personnes qui ont été employées à l'Hôtel-Dieu . . . au service des malades . . . le 15 juin 1788.") On the general background of the Augustine nurses see A. Chevalier, *L'Hôtel-Dieu de Paris et les soeurs augustines, 650 à 1810* (Paris, 1901); J. Boussoulade, *Moniales et hospitalières dans la tourmente révolutionnaire* (Paris, 1962); A. Tenneson, *Les religieuses hospitalières de l'Hôtel-Dieu de Paris, 651 à 1957* (Paris, 1958); *L'Hôtel-Dieu de Paris et ses soeurs augustines, 651 à 1921, par une soeur augustine* (Paris, 1921); D. Weiner, "The French Revolution, Napoleon and the Nursing Profession," *Bulletin of the History of Medicine*, XLV (1972): 274-305; L. S. Greenbaum, "Hospitals, Scientists and Clergy in 18th-Century France: An unpublished Letter of Gaspard Monge to Jacques Tenon on the Hôtel-Dieu of Beaune (1786)," *Episteme* (1975), pp. 51-59.

17. *Mémoire pour les prieure et religieuses hospitalières de l'Hôtel-Dieu de Paris contre Mrs. les administrateurs du temporal dudit Hôtel-Dieu* (Paris 1788), p. 52. (Hereafter *"Mémoire contre les administrateurs."*)

18. Undated letter (September 1787) to Cathedral Chapter of Paris (Bibliothèque Nationale de France, Hereafter "BN"). Manuscrits. Joly de Fleury 1211, fols. 159-64; *Mémoire contre les administrateurs*, p. 62.

19. "Perish the murderous system born in this selfish century, whereby the

teaching hospital which brought in many outsiders at once as dispensary patients and as surgical students.[20] They resisted new reforms of economy and efficiency which transformed the hospital in their eyes into a "tax farm,"[21] and which divested them of their authority. With contempt for the inexperience, arrogance, and dubious remedies of the medical team, which was now to supervise their every move, they attributed far higher efficacy to their consoling ministry, a clear recognition of the importance of what today would be recognized as the psychotherapeutic component of healing:

> It is to women and especially to those who by their vocation are devoted to the continual care of the sick to whom is reserved that empire so sweet that nature and religion give them over the sick, that Providence confers on them. Who better than they know how to console despair, to temper chagrin, to calm anxiety . . . constantly at bedside talking, consoling, does she not more often influence healing than the application of medicines that almost never aid nature.[22]

The clash which arose between nurses and doctors between September 1787 and June 1789, when the hospital was placed under the authority of the Revolution, was the inevitable consequence of two conflicting and incompatible views of the hospital and health-care. The Augustinian sisters went to court to block the enforcement of the new regulations which would "medicalize" the Hôtel-Dieu. Hostility and obstructionist tactics hardened into internecine warfare between nurses and doctors, and the governance of the hospital became virtually impossible on the eve of the convocation of the Estates-General. During all this time — and indeed after — the sisters would boycott the July code.

As early as 1756 and again in 1780 the physicians of the Hôtel-Dieu complained bitterly of "deep-rooted abuses" due to the "misguided devotion" of the Augustinian nuns which had

poor are now only admitted into the hospital to prevent their death, and they should be thrown out just as soon as they cease to be afflicted with sickness. No sooner did this opinion find a single partisan than it is already being practiced in the Hôtel-Dieu of Paris. The religious hasten to rise up against these fatal maxims." (*Mémoire contre les administrateurs*, p. 52).
   20. *Délibérations HD*, pp. 239-40.
   21. *Mémoire contre les administrateurs*, p. 44.
   22. BN, Joly de Fleury 1211, fol. 163.

prevented therapeutic success.[23] The sisters, they held, admitted anyone who came to the hospital, whether or not they required medical care. They overfed patients, ignored dietary regimen,[24] disobediently vetoed medication or treatment whose efficacy they disputed. The nurses kept convalescents on as laundry servants who caused enormous trouble and expanse by stealing, trading in food, and preempting the beds of the real sick.

Colombier's "Regulation of Service in the New Wards" was intended not only to remove these abuses but also to institute the most progressive hospital procedures of the day, namely, those developed in the military hospitals of the realm.[25] To overcome the absence of centralization in the hospital and the independence and arbitrariness of twenty-five wards which operated as twenty-five separate hospitals under twenty-five head sisters, the 1787 rules were meant to impose "invariant principles" throughout. Physicians and surgeons would visit at stated intervals and would collaborate in administering and faithfully recording diet, medication and treatment in case records which would serve as the basis of patient care.[26] Surgeons would henceforth supervise the sisters' distribution of balanced meals, based on standard portions and prepared under lay supervision according to dietary needs prescribed in the patients' log. Frequent snacks, soups and cookies were outlawed. Physicians would henceforth admit patients and discharge them promptly upon termination of treatment. Paid domestics would replace

23. *Délibérations HD*, pp. 215-19.

24. This question has been studied by R. Mandrou, "Un problème de diététique à l'Hôtel-Dieu de Paris à la veille de la Révolution," *Actes du 93e Congrès National des Sociétés Savantes (1968). Section d'Histoire Moderne et Contemporaine*, (Paris, 1971), I: 125-37.

25. Particularly the *Ordonnance du roi portant règlement général concernant les hôpitaux militaires du 2 mai 1781* (Paris 1781). Many of these ideas had previously been defined by Colombier in his *Code de médecine militaire pour le service de terre*. (Paris, 1772), II: i-xi, 1-142 and his *Médecine militaire ou traité des maladies*, (Paris 1778), I: 74-116. See J. des Cilleuls, "Un réformateur de l'hygiène militaire sous l'ancien régime. Jean Colombier, Inspecteur général des hôpitaux (1736-1789)," *La France Médicale*, (1907), LIV: 409-11 and J. des Cilleuls, J. Hassenforder et al., *Le service de santé militaire des ses origines à nos jours* (Paris, 1961), pp. 73-74.

26. Patient case records in seven columns (name, bed, diet, medication, treatment, and discharge) [*Délibérations HD*, p. 186] was based on Colombier, *Code de médecine militaire*, II: 142 ff. See *Ordonnance du roi . . . du 2 mai 1781*, p. 24.

convalescents in discharging housekeeping duties. Lay nurses of both sexes would be assigned to patients by specified ratios to share with nuns and surgeons the care of the sick.[27] Food preparation would be subject to rigorous supervision and economy.

Deprived of their prerogatives in feeding, managing, and discharging the sick, of alone determining which patients the doctors would visit, and executing their verbal orders, the sisters would also lose the direction of their three strongholds in the hospital, the pharmacy, kitchens, and laundry.[28] In an age of serious inflationary rises in the cost of goods and services, food alone amounted to 60 per cent of total hospital expenditures.[29] No wonder that most abuses charged to the sisters had food-cost as their basic concern: control of the kitchens and laundry, meal production and distribution, discharge of convalescents — precisely the articles of the 1787 code most objectionable to the sisters.

It was the first-surgeon Desault whom the Augustinians most immediately identified as the instigator of the July rules and their disseminator not only in the new wing, where they were to be applied provisionally, but in the old wing as well. The man who became the implacable foe of the sisters was the key ally both of the hospital administration and the government. After a brilliant career as professor and head-surgeon of the leading schools and hospitals of Paris,[30] Desault's arrival at the Hôtel-Dieu placed

27. Délibérations HD, p. 220. See J. Tenon, *Mémoires sur les hôpitaux de Paris* (Paris, 1788), p. 131.

28. Already on December 12 1781 a new organization of the pharmacy deprived the sisters of control of that department (*Délibérations HD*, pp. 119-21). On February 21 1787 a "head of laundry" was appointed for a new centralized laundry funded by the government (*Délibérations HD*, pp. 176-80, 190). On July 25 1787 the administration named a Controller of Kitchens (Archives des Religieuses Augustines de l'Hôtel-Dieu de Paris [Hereafter "ARAHD"], "Souvenirs et Notes de la Communauté des religieuses Augustines *hospitalières de l'Hôtel-Dieu de Paris*," (1615-1787), II: fol. 329.

29. Costs of wine, flour, bakery, and kitchens amounted to £830,289 out of a total expenditure of £1,339,474. (Dérouville, *Compte général des recettes et dépenses de l'Hôtel-Dieu de Paris pendant trente-neuf années commencé le premier janvier 1750 et fini le 31 décembre 1788 avec l'état des revenus de l'Hôtel-Dieu* (Paris, 1789), pp. 16-19.

30. P. Huard, "Pierre Desault (1738-1795), Chirurgien de l'Hôtel-Dieu, Professeur de l'Ecole de Santé de Paris," in *Biographies médicales et scientifiques* (Paris, 1972), pp. 119-80 with complete bibliography.

him at the summit of his profession. Its surgery wards performed more operations than any other hospital in Europe.[31] It was here that Desault revolutionized the teaching of surgery.[32] He adroitly reinforced the pride of the hospital administration to make the Hôtel-Dieu the foremost surgical school of Europe.[33] With equal vigor Desault abetted the reform initiative of Colombier by organizing a surgical clinic which after September 1787 combined newly constituted wards, a new amphitheater for operations and clinical instruction, a dissection room and a dispensary for the treatment of the public.[34]

The explosions in the hospital between nurses and doctors in the two years before the French Revolution came as a result of the nuns' attempts to prevent the execution of Desault's reforms. During this period the first-surgeon merged the four wards of the second floor of the old wing into a consolidated surgical service, modelled on a similar obstetrical unit designed by Colombier in the same wing shortly before, and financed in part by the government anxious to see the July rules implemented throughout the hospital.[35] The administration approved Desault's plans for an expanded surgical service in the St. Paul ward by the demolition of partitions, small rooms and the chapel. They accorded equal support to his attempt to end abuses in admission, discharge and police in the ward occasioned by the nuns' "principle of charity." One-third of the 320 male

31. Tenon, *Mémoires sur les hôpitaux de Paris*, p. 223.
32. X. Bichat, *Notice historique sur la vie de Pierre-Joseph Desault* (Paris 1795), pp. 12-14. See J. Rochard, *Histoire de la chirurgie française au XIXe siècle* (Paris, 1875), pp. 5-8.
33. *Délibérations HD*, p. 247.
34. In a letter of November 12 1791 to the National Assembly of the Revolution, Desault claimed that more "real surgeons" were produced in his school in four years than during the previous century in the Hôtel-Dieu. Letter reproduced in T. Gelfand, "A Confrontation over Clinical Instruction at the Hôtel-Dieu of Paris during the French Revolution," *Journal of the History of Medicine and Allied Sciences*, XXVIII (1973): 272. For the dissection room, see p. 275.
35. September 21 1787 (AAPP Registre HD 1787, fol. 631). See August 17 and September 5, 1787 in AN F¹⁵ 233; Registre HD 1787, August 31 and September 5, fols. 595, 602; Registre HD 1787, fols. 6-7, January 2 and *Délibérations HD*, pp. 222, 227; November 26, 1788 in Registre HD 1787 fol. 606. Desault received government support in the provision of single beds supplied by Colombier and later by Necker (September 21 1787, Registre HD 1787, fol. 631; November 14 1788, Registre HD 1788, fol. 590).

surgery patients retained by the sisters, Desault reported, suffered from no surgical maladies.[36] The nuns' continued defiance of dietary regulations impeded surgical treatment.[37] The surgeons could not make their rounds without encountering the sisters' feedings: 5:30 A.M. soup; 9:00 wine; 9:45 meat (called "dinner"); 12:30 snack; 3:00 P.M. bread; 4:00 wine; 4:45 meat or soup; between 8:00 and 9:00 snack and boiled eggs.

The sisters' riposte to each of Desault's proposals was instantaneous and uncompromising. In September and October 1787 they directed letters to their spiritual superiors, the Cathedral Chapter; to the Attorney-General of the Paris parlement; to the Controller-General of Finances and to the King's First-Minister protesting their thousand-year rights within the hospital, "the whole edifice of authority and possession, perhaps the most ancient in the universe."[38] They asked the king to pass a decree of his Royal Council to nullify the July rules. When the sisters were informed that Louis XVI approved those regulations and requested the sisters' compliance,[39] as did their spiritual superiors[40] as well as their temporal masters, the hospital trustees, they threatened appeal to the parlement. In these letters and in future statements, private and public, the sisters decried the surgeons' disrespect, their meddling, degrading surveillance, dictation, immorality, altercations with physicians, neglect and cruelty to patients, professional incompetence, and malpractice.

Since no authority, spiritual or temporal, would support the sisters' appeal, their lawyers proceeded to lodge a writ of summons before the Paris parlement on December 12 1787.[41] In it they demanded the return of their control over the pharmacy, kitchens, laundry and wards, the appointment and discharge of all domestic personnel and nurses, the power to command the

---

36. *Délibérations HD*, pp. 226-27.

37. Ibid, pp. 241-42.

38. Letter October 16 1787 from sisters to Controller-General of Finances (AN, F[15] 233).

39. Letter October 19 1787 from Controller-General to sisters (AN, F[15] 233).

40. AN, "Chapitre de Notre Dame. Délibérations. Année 1787" (LL 232[40(2)]. December 14, 1787, fol. 209, 213.

41. BN. Joly de Fleury 1211, fols. 168-69.

surgeons, and the right to share with the administration complete legislative, managerial and financial authority.

In January 1788 the sisters published a widely-read sixty-four-page memorandum in which they represented themselves as "saints and angels . . . servants of the poor," victimized by an administration which had concocted the July code to "degrade and destroy" them.[42] The memorandum whetted widespread public distrust of the administration[43] (whom the sisters contemptuously addressed as "businessmen of the administration") by accusing them of falsifying financial and patient records and causing the dramatic increase in mortality from 1 in 6 to 1 in 4 (25 per cent). The sisters welcomed the scheme of the four new hospitals, which the administration vigorously opposed, and which they offered to serve. They decried the "tyrannical despotism" of the surgeons who seduced novices and patients, mocked religion and clergy, were noisy and disruptive, and who discharged patients uncured.[44] As for the physicians, they rushed through their rounds, spent between eighteen and twenty seconds with each patient, and altogether failed in their obligation to prescribe adequate treatment.

Against the two powers of the hospital, the administration and the medical staff, the sisters exalted their authority as equals:

> What the administrators are for the temporal, the sisters are for the internal order, the former the management of property, the latter the patients; the former procure aid, the latter divide it; the voice of man chooses the former, religion calls the latter.[45]

> . . . To the physician belongs the visit and treatment of patients, to the surgeon the dressing of their wounds, to the

42. *Mémoire contre les administrateurs,* pp. 62, 16.

43. [Regnier] *Projet d'un Hôpital de Malades ou Hôtel-Dieu* (London and Paris, 1776), pp. 12-14; Abbé de Recalde, *Traité sur les abus qui subsistent dans les hôpitaux du royaume et les moyens propres à les réformer* (Paris, 1786), pp. 4-21; Rondonneau de La Motte, *Essai historique sur l'Hôtel-Dieux de Paris* (Paris, 1787), pp. 131-225.

44. "The Hôtel-Dieu is no longer recognizable in the wards where the young [surgeons] have been admitted . . . rest, silence, calm have been transformed into authority, threats, licentious utterances . . . bacchanalia." (*Mémoire contre les administrateurs,* pp. 37, 55).

45. Ibid, p. 16.

pharmacist the distribution of drugs and to the religious the admission, care and management [of the sick].[46]

Privately the Prioress reported that Desault had countenanced and even abetted the immoral activity of the surgeon apprentices. Nearly all his operations for hernia and lithotomy, she continued, proved fatal. More surgery patients died during the last three years under Desault than had during ten years under his predecessor, J.-N. Moreau,[47] who had accorded the Augustinians full reign over patients.[48] The slightest wounds now take months to heal where before they had taken one week. Finally, she reported, Desault refused to go to mass and interfered not only with religious ceremonies in the wards but also with the administration of the sacraments.

The issue of single beds, fundamental to Desault's ward design, to rational treatment and case-recording, as opposed to the confusion of several patients in the same bed, brought the First-Surgeon into sharp conflict with the Augustinians. The nuns opposed single beds because they believed them to take up nearly as much room as the large ones in which four to six patients could be accommodated. Unsympathetic with Desault's conviction that "health is the principal object in the design of a ward,"[49] they opposed his consolidation of the surgery wards in which fewer patients would take up more space. Desault's reforms coincided with the 1788/89 winter of bitter cold and hunger,[50] which occasioned unprecedented admissions and crowding. On the sisters' recommendations in December 1788 the administration ordered single beds to be replaced by large ones in the fever and obstetrical wards,[51] and elsewhere as urgency required.[52]

46. Ibid, p. 37.

47. Notes of the Prioress to the Attorney-General of the Paris parlement, March 8 1788 and others undated (BN, Joly de Fleury, 1211, fols. 250-52).

48. The sisters approved of Moreau who had acknowledged the Augustinians' "experienced tact" in according them full rights of feeding the sick (April 12 1781, *Délibérations HD*, p. 102). Moreau, a pious Catholic, wished to be buried in the hospital (April 19 1786, *Délibérations HD*, p. 169).

49. November 26 1788, AAPP Registre HD 1788, fol. 606.

50. F. Braudel and E. Labrousse, *Histoire économique et sociale de la France, 1660-1789* (Paris, 1970), pp. 736-38.

51. December 3, 10, 17, 1788, AAPP Registre HD 1788, fols. 619, 624, 632.

52. Ibid, fol. 632.

Les Religieuses de l'hôtel Dieu de Paris estante a la Riviere.
A. Laueure des Cinq Cents Draps, qui ce fait vne fois le mois, ou touttes
   les meres et nouices si doiuent trouber.
B. les petites lauendieres, lauant les Draps, trois fois le jour. Scanoir
   de puis quatre heures du matin jusqu'à neuf heures, de puis
   midy, jusqu'à deux heures, et de puis quatre heures,
   jusqu'à sept heures du soir.

The religious of the Hôtel-Dieu of Paris at the river, washing bedsheets.

Seventeenth-century print in the Cabinet des Estampes of the Bibliothèque Nationale (Paris) reproduced in C. Tollet, *Les édifices hospitaliers depuis leur origine jusqu'à nos jours.* (Paris, 1892), p. 85.

Hospital religious of the Hôtel-Dieu of Paris in working habit serving the sick.

Abbé Hélyot, *Histoire des ordres monastiques, religieux et militaires et des congrégations séculières.* (Paris, 1721), III: 186.

On December 31 the sisters challenged Desault's unshakeable adherence to the single beds by demanding their removal from the surgical wards. Once again they levelled charges of malpractice.[53] When these did not succeed, they complained of intolerable noise and disruptive presence of 400-500 surgical students and spectators, whom Desault had courted by notices in the *Journal de Paris*,[54] and who crowded an amphitheatre built to accommodate 150. The sisters demanded that the use of the amphitheatre, the central component of Desault's teaching and surgical reforms, be drastically cut back. Since women patients, they alleged, had been forcibly brought to the amphitheatre for operations and died as a result of violence, they should no longer be treated there.

With volcanic asperity and in exhaustive detail Desault refuted all these charges on March 31 1789.[55] An investigation of April 2 ordered by the administration found no grounds for malpractice and vindicated the propriety of Desault's conduct and success of his operations. It recommended that the use of the amphitheatre not be curtailed, "because it was useful for the progress of surgical science."[56] The Prioress had ignored the testimony of the surgery-ward sisters who defended the First-Surgeon.[57] "Christian charity forbids the suspicion that the Prioress knew the truth and betrayed it in the intent to harm M. Desault."[58]

On May 6 1789, after all appeals were exhausted, the Prioress notified the administration that her nuns would physically prevent the entry of workmen into the St. Paul ward.[59] This act of defiance was the culmination of a policy of opposition

53. Ibid, fol. 656.

54. *Délibérations HD*, pp. 239-40. The notice in question was published on March 19 1789 (*Journal de Paris*, § 78, p. 360). "M. Desault will begin a course on practical surgery in the amphitheatre of the Hôtel-Dieu today, the nineteenth, in the morning and will continue each day." Desault published similar notices in the *Journal de Paris* on October 8 1787 (p. 1215) and October 2 1786 (p. 1137).

55. *Délibérations HD*, pp. 240-45.

56. Ibid, pp. 245-49.

57. The head sister of the surgical ward remarked that the Prioress and some of her colleagues who were most ardent in bringing suit against the hospital "will ruin the hospital with their fibs." (*Délibérations HD*, p. 248).

58. Ibid, p. 248.

59. Ibid, p. 250.

serious enough for the administration to concede the next day
that internal discipline had broken down inside the hospital, and
for the First-Minister of the king, Jacques Necker himself, to
intervene one week later.[60]

What lay behind the sisters' "unreasonable conduct"? (The
phrase is Necker's.) The answer must be sought in the sisters'
conception of nursing as defined by their constitution
promulgated in 1652 and revised in 1724,[61] the document
constantly cited in their public statements. While the constitution is a list of regulations, it is at the same time the precept
of their faith and rule, a body of ideals which they were to study
each day, to excerpt in writing and to practice (fol. 9).

The life and nursing vocation of the Augustinian nuns of the
Hôtel-Dieu were devoted to purely spiritual ends. Their world
was shaped by evangelical, sacramental, mystical, and symbolic
forces. Nursing was a conscious imitation of the life and works of
Christ whose charitable qualities the nurses were exhorted to
practice. Each act was a gesture of devotion dedicated to the
sacred person of Jesus whom they saw "suffering and languishing
in that of the sick person":

> The hospital religious . . . have a particular obligation to
> honor Our Lord, because He must be the sole and unique
> object of their charity and mercy, and the assistance and
> service which they render the sick and all the charitable
> duties of hospitality must have for their end and principal
> purpose not at all the person of the sick man but the sacred
> person of Jesus. (fol. 177)

Convinced that the health of the soul was more important than
that of the body, and that works of spiritual charity were "more
lofty and more meritorious than corporeal," their objective was
to seek personal salvation through nursing, "through the
exercises of the hospital life to the perfection of the religious
life."

60. BN. Joly de Fleury 1211, fols. 292-293. Reprinted in A. Tuetey,
L'Assistance publique à Paris pendant la Révolution. Documents inédits.
(Paris, 1895), I: 104-5.

61. ARAHD, "Constitutions Faites en 1652 pour les Religieuses de l'Hôtel-
Dieu de Paris par le Chapitre de Paris leur Supérieur et revues en 1725." (578
fols.) Citations in the text hereafter will be given by folio number in parentheses).

The Augustinian nun's view of the sick man and her responsibility to him was taken from Matthew 25:34 where Christ said:

Come the blessed of my Father, take possession of the kingdom prepared for you since the beginning of the world. Because I was hungry you fed me. I was thirsty and you gave me to drink. I was received by you as a guest and traveller and you showed me holy hospitality. Frequently I appeared before you naked and you clothed me. You saw me with the infirmities of sickness and with sores and you visited me. To put it in one word: Blessed are the merciful because they will receive mercy. (fol. 22)

The novice took four vows after an apprenticeship of six years, the three customary vows of poverty, chastity and obedience, and a fourth for the care of the sick. At every turn the sisters were chastened to their redoubtable responsibilities for the welfare of the sick by the promise of spiritual reward or punishment:

. . . the slightest service rendered [the sick], He [Christ] will consider done to His own person, and a glass of water given the sick with this spirit and this intention on earth will merit eternal reward in heaven. (fol. 177)

If by absence or neglect the sick should suffer some notable loss of health or some interested motive regarding the salvation of their soul [the sisters] will answer for it before God who will demand a very exact accounting at the hour of their death of service and charity due to their fault and negligence. (fol. 99)

Each nursing obligation was a symbolic reenactment of a religious or scriptural act, a compound of serving and saving. In admitting the sick the sisters evoked Christ's injunction, "Come to me all who suffer."[62] As many poor as the hospital could contain were to be admitted, "since charity is limitless and impartial." The sisters' first obligation was to assign the sick man to a ward and procure one of the twenty-four priests to confess him. They delivered the new admission to his bed, undressed him

---

62. *Exercise du jour pour les religieuses de l'Hôtel-Dieu de Paris* (Paris, 1637), p. 27.

with modesty and kindness, washed his feet and kissed them. While undressing the patient the sisters exhorted him to place himself well in the eyes of God, "the first and sovereign doctor," and to suffer illness with resignation in conformity to God's will, to adopt a proper frame of mind to receive both spiritual and corporeal assistance. The sisters then furnished each patient clean linen, as Christ had, cut his nails, washed his hands and gave him a fresh chamber pot which they emptied regularly. Each sister was obliged to answer the call of the sick "as to the voice of Jesus Christ, her husband."

The bed was the symbol of divine mercy and the center of the sisters' spiritual vocation. It was the place where their obligations both to God and the sick were discharged. Changing the bed was a religious exercise, a chance to give thanks for surviving the night, to remind the sick to suffer affliction and inconvenience for the love of God. In returning the sick to their beds, the sisters were to ask them to recite the Pater, Ave Maria, and the Credo.

The nurses' spiritual obligations at bedside were considerable. It was their responsibility to see that the sick confessed and communicated. The sisters were to "teach the ignorant theology necessary for salvation," the mysteries of the faith, the teachings of Christ and the apostles, the meaning of the eucharist and transsubstantiation, the commandments, prayers, catechism, confession, communion, and devotion to Mary. Their attentions were to go out equally to heretics, infidels, and unwed mothers, seeking whenever possible "sincere conversions," preparing patients to receive the sacraments, instilling love and fear of God with the view of securing penitence and moral rehabilitation. The sisters led patients in prayers, in acts of adoration and contrition. Feeding was a conscious reenactment of the Lord's Supper. At 9:30 and 5:00 when bread and wine were distributed, the patient's hands and mouth were washed. The sick were turned to face the crucifix and were led in various prayers of benediction. While the only washing of patients mentioned in the constitution was the hands, mouth, and feet, these essentially religious acts were also hygenically beneficial. The sisters also prepared patients for death and interment, conceiving themselves as the Virgin and the Three Maries readying Christ for burial in the person of the poor, cleansing the sacred wounds and kissing them. (fol. 498)

It would be difficult to exaggerate the hard life of the Augustinian nurses and the unspeakable conditions in the ancient hospital under which they worked. Their day began upon rising at 4:00 A.M. and lasted until 9:00 at night. Ten times during the day they left the wards for religious observances in the convent: mass, prayers, spiritual exercises, sermons, confessions, examination of conscience, chapter meetings, meals in the refectory, and daily meditation of the rule. Subjected to contagious diseases and occasionally to epidemics which swept through the hospital, and to which some fell victim, they faced death, like the martyrdom of Christ, as the highest dignity of their calling, "adding the lily of their virginal purity to the glorious palm of the martyr." It was only the vision of Christ, a sublime faith and other-worldliness which they carried back to the wards from their ceremonial observances and religious rites that made the conditions of the hospital bearable. How else suffer the rending sight of the ailing poor, most reduced to rags, many aged, deformed, hungry, homeless, jobless, often without family or friends, unwashed, stinking, coarse, covered with lice and sores, bringing to the hospital as their sole legacy the full panoply of disease — except as the "sacred humanity of Jesus."[63]

And how else support the crushing drudgery of hospital routine, day in and day out, amid the dismal hygienic conditions of the Hôtel-Dieu,[64] the terrible crowding of patients in the same beds, the noise, congestion, total absence of privacy, the lack of adequate facilities, space, heat in winter, ventilation in summer, decent living quarters for nurses and personnel forced to live in the wards. How else support poor food, the perpetual stench of slop pails and privies more conspicuous for their filth and nauseous odor than their operational efficiency. The absence of running water found the sisters and their domestic staff obliged to wash 2400 soiled sheets[65] and piles of other hospital linen each day in the waters of the Seine or in tiny rooms adjoining the

63. ". . . those to whom was promised the kingdom of the heavens . . . who will receive crowns and rewards . . . in the bosom of God himself who will shower them all the more with happiness and glory for having suffered pain and contempt in the world." (fol. 496).

64. This subject is considered at length in L. S. Greenbaum, " 'Measure of Civilisation': The Hospital Thought of Jacques Tenon on the Eve of the French Revolution," *Bulletin of the History of Medicine*, XLIX (1975): 43-56.

65. *Délibérations HD*, p. 176.

wards. The perpetual reminder that Christ, too, had endured "torments and tortures" was their strength. The nuns were placed under the continual obligation to mortify the flesh, never to give in to feelings of repugnance and disgust, remembering that virtue and perfection were not acquired without difficulty (fol. 449), sharing a loathing for the body which found itself continually in contest with the spirit.[66] Only the continual living of their vows sustained them in the performance of otherwise revolting tasks like bathing the sick, holding their heads while they vomited, changing their beds, cleaning their soiled linen, emptying their slops, suffering their curses, blows and abuses — tasks which the thirteenth-century Cardinal de Vitry had already described:

> The sisters endured with cheerfulness and without repugnance the stench, the filth and infections of the sick, so insupportable to others, that no other form of penitence could be compared to this species of martyrdom. No one who saw the religious sisters of the Hôtel-Dieu not only do dressings, make beds and bathe patients, but also in cold winter break the ice in the river Seine and stand knee-deep in the water to wash the filthy clothes, could regard them as other than holy victims, who from excess of love and charity for their neighbors hastened willingly to the death which they courted amidst the stenches and infections.[67]

The nuns were probably quite correct in feeling themselves infinitely superior to secular nurses and orderlies who came and went in the hospital, and who did not enjoy the Augustinians' reputation for dedication or kindness to the sick.

As a final tribute to the Augustinian nurses it must be remembered that the hospital sisters were cloistered nuns who quit the world and their loved ones as young girls, who spent their entire lives in the hospital atmosphere — and many gave forty, fifty or sixty years of service (the median service was thirty-four years),[68] cut away from all outside rewards for their labors,

---

66. ". . . considering much more the necessities of the soul created in the image and semblance of God and destined for eternity, not that of the body which is nothing but terrestrial." (fol. 443).

67. Abbé Hélyot, *Histoire des ordres monastiques religieux et militaires et des congrégations séculières*, (Paris, 1721), III: 185. Quoted in M. A. Nutting and L. L. Dock, *A History of Nursing*, (New York, 1935), I: 303-04.

68. See Appendix II.

who were forbidden to leave the hospital except by permission on rare nursing assignments elsewhere and who suffered the rancor, pettiness and frustration of their fellow sisters.[69] While only their profound faith and zeal for the perfection of their spiritual vocation made their job possible, these very same attributes accounted for their insularity, made them distrustful of change within the hospital, rendered them jealous of their authority, unshakable in the conviction of their exclusive right and prerogatives and unafraid of secular power.

In the light of these ideals and their published statements it is clear that piety lay at the heart of their quarrels with the doctors. In 1788 they wrote:

> The sisters have received, treated and healed [the sick] . . . this is almost always a scene of gratitude and effusion. Kneeling before the feet of their benefactress and giving thanks to Providence before its dearest image . . . For the religious this is the amount of most perfect happiness. Is there an enjoyment sweeter than being able to say as Our Divine Savior, *"Go, you are cured."* And now the religious are deprived of it.[70]

Patients are now callously "thrown out" on the orders of the surgeons, discharged like the dove of Noah's ark, "not knowing where to alight, they soon return."[71]

> Before, the distribution of food was accomplished with decency, cleanliness and a sort of majesty. The sisters distributed bread, soup, wine . . . and meat in the image of Providence who distributes His gifts to His children.

69. A Rousselet *Notes sur l'ancien Hôtel-Dieu de Paris relatives à la lutte des administrateurs laïques contre le pouvoir spirituel* (Paris, 1888) details the petulance and ugliness of the sisters within their community. It is a work which must be used with caution. See also Desault's description: ". . . quarrelling constantly, the sisters, not being able to secure either respect or obedience from the servants who reply insolently, fight with each other and quarrel with the patients and mistreat them. The patients themselves sing, whistle, smoke in their beds undeterred by anyone. There is not a single second that goes by without hearing either a head sister who asks for convalescents, another who shouts after a laundry boy, an attendant who calls out at the top of her lungs throughout the entire ward the name of a patient being sought in order to learn where he is sleeping, a sister who shouts 'who wants some bouillon?', etc. . . ." (*Délibérations HD*, p. 243).

70. *Mémoire contre les administrateurs*, p. 4.

71. Ibid, p. 6.

Whatever she presented was received with gratitude . . . to
edify virtuous souls, the poor, the friends of the sick. [Now
food is] thrown at the sick without consulting their taste,
chance governs their lot . . . the sick are treated like
prisoners.[72]

Unable and unwilling to see patient-care as an exclusively
clinical function, it followed that the hospital as a purely curative
institution was equally abhorrent to the sisters.[73]

That the struggle between doctors and nurses should have
proved so protracted — in defiance of the expressed disapproval
both of the Augustinians' spiritual and temporal superiors,
ministers of state and the king himself — was due to the universal
admiration of the nuns' piety, to the absence of any clearly-
defined coercive authority within the hospital and the nearly
insurmountable power of tradition, and to powerful protection
among hospital trustees and the parlement in the person of Omer
Joly de Fleury, attorney-general of the Paris parlement, trustee
and legal guardian of the Hôtel-Dieu. Joly de Fleury was the
third generation of an eminent magisterial clan to hold that post
during the century,[74] a family which held close ties of sentiment
and friendship to the Augustinians.[75] The sisters considered the
parlement their "direct protector" and were feverish partisans of
the *thèse nobiliaire* in the parlement's struggles with the crown.[76]
They conferred Christ's title "Father of the Poor" on Joly de
Fleury,[77] who, in turn, sympathized with their plight, tried to
work out a compromise, attempted to whittle down the power of
Desault and the surgeons, and even to postpone their reforms.[78]

72. Ibid, p. 38.
73. See note § 12.

74. A Molinier, *Inventaire sommaire de la collection Joly de Fleury* (Paris,
1881), pp. vi-viii; C. Bloch, *Inventaire sommaire de la collection Joly de Fleury
concernant l'assistance et la mendicité* (Paris, 1908), p. 5.

75. ARAHD. "Mémoires sur la vie de la Mère de la Miséricorde, Religieuse
de l'Hôtel-Dieu de Paris (1767)," manuscript note at end of Volume II; *Institut
des religieuses de l'Hôtel-Dieu de Paris (VIIe au XXe siècle)*. One predecessor
of Joly de Fleury was the author of the sisters' revised constitution of 1725
(Fosseyeux, *L'Hôtel-Dieu de Paris*, p. 32).

76. Letter of the Prioress, October 6 1788 (BN, Joly de Fleury 1211, fol.
165).

77. Letter of the Prioress, December 25 1787 (BN, Joly de Fleury 1211, fol.
174).

78. Letter of Joly de Fleury to the hospital administration, February 16

Known for mediocrity and incapacity,[79] Joly de Fleury lived up to his reputation. He humored the sisters, left dangling a hospital administration brought to the verge of resignation and stymied by the unparalleled challenge of the sisters,[80] delayed the trial interminably, and exasperated everyone. The final result was a no-win game. Overwhelming medical arguments had convinced the Attorney-General that the governing authority of the hospital must remain with the administration, and that the July regulations could not be revoked.[81] Yet nothing short of revocation would have satisfied the sisters. While it was known in Paris,[82] and seriously pondered by Joly de Fleury,[83] that continued disobedience might cause the Augustinians to be replaced in the Hôtel-Dieu by the Sisters of Charity, who by the training of their founder, Saint Vincent de Paul, were obedient to doctors' orders,[84] such a transformation would have been difficult to accomplish.

The authority which Joly de Fleury may have had to force the sisters' obedience — and he was appealed to by administration, Archbishop of Paris, Chapter, lawyers, medical

1788 (BN, Joly de Fleury 1211, fol. 191).

79. "Notoriously, infinitely below the requirements of that office, as much by ignorance and incapacity which have occasioned dissipations of all kinds." (S. P. Hardy, "Mes loisirs ou journal d'événemens, tels qu'ils parviennent à ma connaissance," [BN, Manuscrits Français 6686, 1787-1788, VII: fol. 318]); "He brought to the parlement the most complete and indeed the most unpleasant mediocrity ever seen." Mémoires du comte Beugnot ancien ministre [1783-1815], A. Beugnot, ed., (Paris, 1866), I: 53.

80. Délibérations HD, p. 230.

81. BN, Joly de Fleury 1211, fol. 186 ("Réflexions," January 1788).

82. BN, Hardy, "Mes Loisirs," March 18 1788, VII: fol. 392.

83. BN, Joly de Fleury 1211, fol. 187.

84. "You should act, my sisters, with great respect and obedience towards the doctors, taking great care never to condemn or contradict their orders. Endeavor on the contrary to fulfill them with great exactitude and without ever presuming to prepare the medicines according to your own way of thinking. Punctually follow what they have prescribed both with regard to the quantity of the dose and the ingredients of which it is composed, because upon this fidelity and exactness depends nothing less perhaps than the life of the patient. Respect the doctors not only because they are more learned and enlightened than you but because God commands you in the Holy Scriptures to do so in the following words, 'Honor the Physicians for the need thou hast of them.' " Quoted in Nutting and Dock, A History of Nursing, I: 424. A slightly different version may be read in the original, "Premières explications sur le règle, 14 juin 1642," in Conférences de St. Vincent de Paul aux filles de la charité (Paris, 1881), p. 55.

staff and Necker — he lost by ineffectiveness. In June 1789 the sisters threw over their only friend by a second printed memorandum in which they announced that the Attorney-General must disqualify himself from their case which both plaintiffs and defendants now wished promptly judged.[85] Joly de Fleury's only success — if success it was — was to secure a prolonged delay of the trial, which he acknowledged would have proved very damaging to the sisters, and which was subsequently laid aside at the Revolutionary reorganization of the hospital two months later.[86] By the time the Revolution erupted the sisters had succeeded in alienating everyone — crown, government, Chapter, Archbishop, hospital administration, trustees, doctors, secular nurses, public opinion. But the pious and fearless Augustinian sisters believed God to be on the side of righteousness, and this was sufficient justification to stick unyieldingly to their position.[87]

* * * * *

The Augustinian nuns and Desault championed two competing "faiths," piety and medicine with the ardor of true believers. Each heaped scorn on the feeble competence of the other, and in very nearly similar terms.[88] Each considered the other "mercenaries."[89] Each held education as a central preoccupation, Christian revelation and faith to the nurses, clinical instruction to the doctors. Each claimed sovereign

85. *Mémoire pour les prieure et religieuses hospitalières de l'Hôtel-Dieu de Paris contre M. le procureur général* (Paris, 1789), 8 pp. A copy may be found in BN, Joly de Fleury 1217, fols. 201-4.

86. Délibérations HD, pp. 253-254. Cf. M. Fosseyeux, "L'Hôtel-Dieu de Paris sous la Révolution (1789-1802)," *La Révolution Français*, (1914), LXVI: 40-85.

87. "Courage can only belong to generous hearts, which is their richest patrimony, only to flaming souls of the divine fire who are no longer on earth or who remain only by bonds of an ardent charity which danger cannot break without the aid of death." (*Délibérations HD*, p. 291).

88. "the so-called knowledge" (*Mémoire contre les administrateurs*, p. 7); "their so-called service," (Desault in *Délibérations HD*, p. 241).

89. *Mémoire contre les administrateurs*, p. 62. The relationship of surgeons to sisters was "the servant raised above the master, the wage-earner above the owner." (*Mémoire contre les administrateurs*, p. 29); "mercenary hands" (Desault, *Prospectus de l'Ecole de chirurgie, établie au Grand Hospice d'Humanité* [Paris, n.d.], AN, AD. VIII, 30, p. 2).

jurisdiction over patients by appeal to philanthropic philosophies, religious charity, on the one hand, secular welfare (*bienfaisance*) on the other.[90] Desault contended that the reasons the sisters "are angry is that [he] . . . can do more good than they,"[91] an obvious reference to the superior efficacy of medicine. Desault's charge to his surgical students at the Hôtel-Dieu "to look after and console the sick,"[92] was a responsibility not unlike that pressed on the Augustinian nuns by their religious constitution, but one which subsumed the nursing function under the mantle of the surgical practitioner. According to one of his students at the Hôtel-Dieu,[93] Desault commanded the nurses along the entire course of nursing services, and down to fine details — feeding, admission, ward assignment, undressing the sick, making their beds and placing them inside, the number of nurses on duty, and the manner in which they exercised hospitality — "in fact everything connected to the health of the sick." Little wonder that nurses and doctors of the Paris hospital after 1787 were locked in what La Rochefoucauld-Liancourt's Poverty Committee reported was "intestine warfare . . . an odious struggle between these two authorities."[94]

The struggle for the mastery of the hospital, for this is what really was at issue between nurses and doctors, settled by some reductionist logic on the bed, the epitome of two contradictory persuasions. For the sisters it was the sacramental setting within which to practice piety, to instruct, to inspire, to convert, to fill with as many needy as possible. To the doctors, it was the indispensable resort of each patient's rest and rehabilitation, the space where controlled treatment and clinical teaching could be practiced from precise data recorded *in situ*.[95] While formal

90. Desault considered himself "an honest soul doing good" (*Délibérations HD*, p. 244).

91. Ibid, p. 244.

92. Desault, *Prospectus*, p. 2.

93. Marc-Antoine Petit (1766-1811), "Eloge de Pierre-Joseph Desault, chirurgien-en-chef de l'Hôtel-Dieu de Paris," in *Essai sur la médecine du coeur* (Lyon, 1806), p. 107.

94. *Procès-Verbaux et rapports du comité de mendicité de la Constituante 1790-1791*, C. Bloch and A. Tuetey, eds. (Paris, 1911), pp. 641, 644.

95. See E. Coyecque, "Consultations de Desault chirurgien en chef de l'Hôtel-Dieu, 1786-1787," *Bulletin de la Soc. de l'Hist. de Paris et l'Ile de France*, XXXVII (1910): 254-56.

nursing education was still a century away in France,[96] the 1787 regulations saw the first secularization of nursing by the appointment of lay nurses who shared responsibility with the sisters. It also set dietary standards of French hospitals legislated in 1806.[97] Both the supervisory function of the wards and the residual elements of health care still in the hands of the sisters would eventually be surrendered to the medical team at whose head the doctor stood. But this did not happen overnight, and reports of the Augustinians' persisting abuses and continuing tyranny rang out during the French Revolution.[98] As late as the Third French Republic medical reformers bent on professionalizing nurses, like Dr. D.-M. Bourneville, founder of the *Année médicale*, still berated the nuns (who remained in the Hôtel-Dieu until 1908) for their ancient ways:

> The religious, nurse of the soul, is the auxiliary of the priest. The lay nurse, caring for the body, is the auxiliary of the doctor. Because of this, and we cannot blame her, the sister is true to the statutes of her congregation to save the soul first, after which comes the body, if there is still time.

96. See the works of one of its founders, Anna Hamilton, *Considérations sur les infirmières des hôpitaux* (Montpellier, 1900) and A. Hamilton and F. Regnault, *Les gardes-malades, Congréganistes, mercenaires, amateurs, professionelles* (Paris, 1901). Also the excellent treatment, "The Revolution in French Hospitals," in Nutting and Dock, *A History of Nursing*, (New York, 1912), III: 279-340.

97. Mandrou, "Un problème de diététique à l'Hôtel-Dieu," p. 136.

98. See the petition of the servants of the Hôtel-Dieu to the National Assembly on July 1 1791, attempting to defend themselves against the "despotic authority" of the Augustinians, ". . . classing themselves in the ranks of angelic spirits . . . the spirit of charity is totally banished from their language . . ." (*Délibérations HD*, pp. 286-87). See the report of the Revolutionary municipal authority [A.-L. de Jussieu] *Compte rendu à la commune, par le département des hôpitaux* (Paris, 1790), who contended that the sisters still resisted supervision by the doctors in feeding and discharging convalescents and that they "still pretended to reserve to themselves exclusive management" of the sick (pp. 19-20). Much of the same was reported by La Rochefoucauld-Liancourt and the Poverty Committee, ("absolute masters of the policing of the wards.") They concluded: "We cannot refrain from believing that it is principally in the empire that the sisters exercise in the Hôtel-Dieu and their resistance to all authority that must be attributed the perpetuation of several abuses and very great obstacles." (*Procès-verbaux et rapports du comité de mendicité* [pp. 641-42]. Desault conceded two years later in 1792 that nothing had changed (*Prospectus*, p. 7).

Everyone knows that as death approaches the sisters first notify the priest, then the doctor . . .[99]

[As for] the nuns: little time given to the wards; much spent in religious exercise. Little or no personal care given to patients, especially as concerned necessary attentions to the genital zone; refusal to nurse venereal cases, lying-in women, and unmarried mothers. These were left entirely to the servant nurses . . . Meagre respect for administrative rules. The Superior or Prioress came before the physician or the directors; the soul was more important than the body.[100]

Until the end of the Old Regime the sisters continued to see themselves as perhaps they deserved to be remembered in the hospitals — as angels. But visions often become clouded or obstructed, and honest men may dispute the meaning of the term. In rendering judgement on the Augustinian nuns of the Hôtel-Dieu, one is tempted to evoke the experience of Cardinal de Noailles, Archbishop of Paris under Louis XIV a century earlier, who remarked about another group of sisters, the saintly Jansenist nuns of Port Royal, that they were "as pure as angels and as disobedient as devils."[101] It is perhaps fitting to conclude with a haunting admonition handed down to the sisters by the canon authors of their constitution in which the angelic metaphor turned out to be a double-edged sword:

We desire that our dear daughters have much devotion and piety in the service of God, in order that, seeing Him continuously in the persons of the poor sick, they will be inclined to serve them with more respect, fidelity, and love. And we declare that all the prayers and other spiritual exercises that may distract them, however little it may be, from practicing charity to the sick, as required, are temptations of Satan who transforms himself into the angel of light to destroy by this deceiving artifice the spirit of their

99. *Enseignement professionel des infirmières. Laïcisation de l'Assistance publique. Les écoles infirmières* (Paris, 1904), p. 457. See *Laïcisation de l'Assistance publique. Laïques et religieuses* (Paris, n.d.).

100. Quoted in Nutting and Dock, *History of Nursing*, III: 290.

101. W. H. Lewis, *The Splendid Century. Life in the France of Louis XIV* (New York, 1971), p. 88.

vocation which they must cherish as the greatest treasure they possess in the world. (fol. 6).

Louis S. Greenbaum

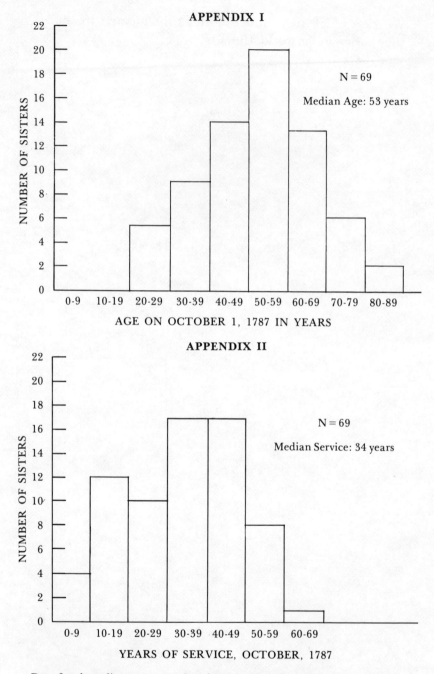

APPENDIX I

NUMBER OF SISTERS (vertical axis, 0–22)

N = 69

Median Age: 53 years

AGE ON OCTOBER 1, 1787 IN YEARS
(0-9, 10-19, 20-29, 30-39, 40-49, 50-59, 60-69, 70-79, 80-89)

APPENDIX II

NUMBER OF SISTERS (vertical axis, 0–22)

N = 69

Median Service: 34 years

YEARS OF SERVICE, OCTOBER, 1787
(0-9, 10-19, 20-29, 30-39, 40-49, 50-59, 60-69)

Data for these diagrams was taken from Archives des religieuses augustines de l'Hôtel-Dieu de Paris, "Notes et Souvenirs," 844 fols.